T0311706

Cambridge Elements ☰

Elements in Magic
edited by
Marion Gibson
University of Exeter

WITCHCRAFT AND THE MODERN ROMAN CATHOLIC CHURCH

Francis Young
Independent Scholar

CAMBRIDGE
UNIVERSITY PRESS

CAMBRIDGE
UNIVERSITY PRESS

University Printing House, Cambridge CB2 8BS, United Kingdom

One Liberty Plaza, 20th Floor, New York, NY 10006, USA

477 Williamstown Road, Port Melbourne, VIC 3207, Australia

314–321, 3rd Floor, Plot 3, Splendor Forum, Jasola District Centre, New Delhi – 110025, India

103 Penang Road, #05–06/07, Visioncrest Commercial, Singapore 238467

Cambridge University Press is part of the University of Cambridge.

It furthers the University's mission by disseminating knowledge in the pursuit of education, learning, and research at the highest international levels of excellence.

www.cambridge.org
Information on this title: www.cambridge.org/9781108948753
DOI: 10.1017/9781108953337

First published 2022

A catalogue record for this publication is available from the British Library.

ISBN 978-1-108-94875-3 Paperback
ISSN 2732-4087 (online)
ISSN 2732-4079 (print)

Witchcraft and the Modern Roman Catholic Church

Elements in Magic

DOI: 10.1017/9781108953337
First published online: January 2022

Francis Young
Independent Scholar

Author for correspondence: Francis Young, francis.young@conted.ox.ac.uk

Abstract: Witchcraft is rarely mentioned in official documents of the contemporary Roman Catholic Church, but ideas about the dangers of witchcraft and other forms of occultism underpin the recent revival of interest in exorcism in the church. This Element examines hierarchical and clerical understandings of witchcraft within the contemporary Roman Catholic Church. It considers the difficulties faced by clergy in parts of the developing world, where belief in witchcraft is so dominant that it has the potential to undermine the church's doctrine and authority. The Element also considers the revival of interest in witchcraft and cursing among Catholic demonologists and exorcists in the developed world. The Element explores whether it is possible for a global church to adopt any kind of coherent approach to a phenomenon appraised so differently across different cultures that the church's responses to witchcraft in one context are likely to seem irrelevant in another.

This Element also has a video abstract: www.cambridge.org/witchcraft

Keywords: Roman Catholicism, witchcraft, sorcery, demonology, exorcism

ISBNs: 9781108948753 (PB), 9781108953337 (OC)
ISSNs: 2732-4087 (online), 2732-4079 (print)

Contents

1 Introduction

The subject of this Element is official and semi-official contemporary attitudes to witchcraft (and to belief in witchcraft) among the clergy of the Roman Catholic Church in the period since the end of the Second Vatican Council in 1965. While many of the world's 1.2 billion Catholics may well believe in some form of witchcraft, the focus of this study is not the vast subject of popular Catholic belief in witchcraft,[1] but rather the ways in which the hierarchy of the Catholic church (and its delegated specialists, the diocesan exorcists) has responded to such beliefs in the modern world. While 'witchcraft' has a variety of meanings in contemporary culture (including positive ones), for the purposes of this Element, 'witchcraft' refers to a belief in the possibility of occult harm caused by or channelled through other human beings, including curses, hexes, the 'evil eye', and other cultural variations on the theme of preternatural harm projected by a third party.

In the process of writing my book *A History of Exorcism in Catholic Christianity*,[2] which was focussed on understanding the historical background to the resurgence of the practice of exorcism within contemporary Catholicism, I became aware that a separate study was needed of the church's current approach to witchcraft. The relationship between the Roman Catholic Church and witchcraft matters because, more than any other aspect of Catholic demonology, it is a site of contestation between official theologies and popular religion. The issue of witchcraft exposes the extent of the church's willingness to accommodate and assimilate culturally specific beliefs about preternatural harm. It is an issue that reveals the competing imperatives of teaching the essentials of the faith without 'superstition' on the one hand and responding to the pastoral needs of the faithful on the other – imperatives that have been in tension since at least the Council of Trent in the sixteenth century. The study of the contemporary church's official and semi-official responses to belief in witchcraft thus offers revealing insights into the operation of authority within the Roman Catholic Church, as well as the ways in which the church negotiates its relationship with the beliefs of the faithful and with its own tradition.

Exorcism and associated practices are the contemporary Catholic church's foremost official response to the presumed presence of spiritual evil, and the practice of exorcism is informed by underlying theoretical demonology that usually acknowledges the possibility of witchcraft. Witchcraft was a relative

---

[1] On belief in witchcraft in contemporary worldwide Catholic cultures, see Boi-Nai and Kirby 1998: 533–53; De Blécourt 1999: 143–219; Green 2003: 120–40; Behrend 2007: 41–58; Zocca and Urame 2008; Lado 2009: 71–92.

[2] Young 2016.

latecomer to Catholic demonology, first appearing as a serious concern of churchmen in the late Middle Ages, but it has historically served an important explanatory purpose in demonology, since it accounts for demonic attacks on the innocent. Early accounts of demonic possession emphasized the demoniac's sin as the cause of demonic activity. In 417, Pope Innocent I referred to 'baptized persons, who are afterwards possessed by a demon on account of some vice or intervening sin'.[3] The idea that demonic vexation of the faithful was the result of sin remained the dominant interpretation until the fifteenth century when witchcraft was adopted by some theologians as an explanation for how innocent people came to experience demonic vexation.[4]

This study approaches the Catholic church's relationship with belief in witchcraft from the perspective of contemporary church history, drawing on documentary evidence such as official Vatican documents, papal locutions, documents authorized by national bishops' conferences, and the writings of priests authorized to function as diocesan exorcists. Although the highest level of the church's official approach to witchcraft is found in liturgical and catechetical documents such as the rite of exorcism and the *Catechism*, canon law entrusts the ministry of exorcism to the diocesan bishop, and therefore, to his discretion and to the discretion of any priest whom the bishop appoints as a diocesan exorcist within the norms of canon law and the liturgical norms of the authorized rites. Responses to the problem of witchcraft in the writings of episcopally authorized exorcists and other clerical demonologists thus express the attitudes of those empowered by the church to deal with demonic activity. While the writings of exorcists on witchcraft represent their personal views and often include individual and cultural idiosyncrasies, they also often reflect the views of the exorcist's bishop and the culture of dealing with witchcraft within a particular nation. Moreover, they reflect the academic formation of would-be exorcists and, often, the nature of the training offered by bodies such as the International Association of Exorcists.

The approach adopted in this Element is by no means exhaustive; the church's relationship with witchcraft belief could also be approached from the perspectives of anthropology, folklore, canon law, theology, and the sociology of religion (and indeed, Giuseppe Giordan and Adam Possamai have recently demonstrated that the practice of exorcism can be approached from a sociological perspective, drawing on interviews, oral testimony, and quantitative data).[5] Even within the limits of published sources, this study cannot be a comprehensive one, since new writings on witchcraft by diocesan exorcists are appearing all the time throughout the world. However, this study sets out to

---

[3] Young 2016: 45.   [4] Young 2016: 68.   [5] Giordan and Possamai 2018

introduce the subject of official and semi-official Catholic approaches to witchcraft by analysing the relevant liturgical and catechetical documents, the approaches of a selection of exorcists from across the world, and major events in the development of contemporary Catholic attitudes to the problems of witchcraft and witchcraft belief. This is a new area of research where a great deal of more work is needed, from the perspectives of multiple disciplines, and the conclusion outlines some potential future directions for research.

All translations from languages other than English are my own, with the exception of quotations from the English edition of Gabriele Amorth's *An Exorcist Tells His Story*.[6]

2 Historical Background

2.1 Defining Witchcraft

The challenge of defining witchcraft is a notoriously difficult problem in historiography, but fortunately, the scope and nature of this Element do not require a single, universally applicable definition of witchcraft. This Element is concerned only with what those authorities might consider 'witchcraft' to be. However, since the term is used quite broadly by some modern Catholic demonologists to mean any form of magic, occultism, esotericism, or even non-Christian spirituality, there is clearly a danger that the term may lose any vestige of meaning at all unless some boundaries are imposed. In fact, the use of 'witchcraft' in such a general way by Catholic demonologists is a very recent phenomenon; historically, what Catholic demonologists called 'witchcraft' invariably included an element of directed supernatural harm. The anthropologist Garrick Bailey's definition of sorcery as 'the performance of rites and spells intended to cause supernatural forces to harm others' broadly corresponds to what Catholic demonologists have traditionally considered witchcraft to be.[7]

Although Bailey goes on to distinguish sorcery from witchcraft, defining witchcraft as 'the use of psychic power alone to cause harm to others',[8] a distinction between sorcery and witchcraft is not usually acknowledged by Catholic demonologists, and the two terms are used interchangeably. The category of 'witchcraft proper' (as opposed to spiritual practices deemed undesirable and labelled *pejoratively* as witchcraft) is still quite an expansive one, including curses, the evil eye, and the casting of spells, but the common characteristics of all witchcraft proper in Catholic demonology are the intent to cause harm and the mediation, in some way or another, of a human agent. This 'witchcraft proper' may be called malefic witchcraft (from the Latin

---

[6] Amorth 1999.   [7] Bailey and Peoples 2013: 265–6.   [8] Bailey and Peoples 2013: 266.

maleficium) to distinguish it from other uses of the term because it is classically directed towards the working of evil.[9] A further feature of witchcraft – and one that may distinguish it from other forms of magic and from sorcery – is its association with the marginalized in society. In most areas of Europe, witchcraft accusations usually targeted women, but on a global scale, gender is not the only factor in witchcraft accusations, not even the dominant factor in some societies.[10] For example, in much of Africa, it is the elderly, the disabled, and children (of either sex) who tend to be accused of witchcraft.[11]

The rarity (or perceived rarity) of traditional malefic witchcraft in large parts of the developed world may be one reason why the term 'witchcraft' is now applied by many Catholic demonologists to various forms of occultism, esotericism, 'New Age' spirituality, and neo-paganism that are ultimately rooted in the occult revival of the late nineteenth century. In many regions of the developing world, by contrast, witchcraft retains its core meaning as directed spiritual harm. This variation in usage of the term exposes the challenge the church faces in formulating a single coherent response to witchcraft and belief in witchcraft across the entire Catholic world, where cultural perceptions of what witchcraft is may be very different. However, as we shall see, the perception that traditional malefic witchcraft is largely a thing of the past in the developed world may be misplaced.

Further difficulties of definition are raised by the fact that every language has its own distinctive term for witchcraft that has specific and sometimes unique cultural associations so that no translation will ever be exact. The problem is illustrated by the fact that even the Italian language, widely used in the Roman Curia and in most cases the successor of Latin, has a term for witchcraft (*stregoneria*) that does not exactly correspond to the Latin terms *maleficium* and *sortilegium* that are normally used in Latin documents referring to witchcraft. In languages unconnected with Latin with only a recent tradition of Catholic theological vocabulary, especially in the developing world, the problem of translation is significantly magnified.

While a church reluctant to discuss witchcraft has long faced the question of how to evangelize societies where belief in witchcraft is particularly intense, the rapid rise of Pentecostalist churches in former strongholds of Catholicism, such as Brazil, has left the Catholic church facing spiritual competition from denominations and styles of Christianity that do not hesitate to affirm the reality and danger of witchcraft. The need for sensitive pastoral responses in societies where belief in witchcraft is widespread is complicated by an additional

---

[9] Young 2017: 13.   [10] Clark 1997: 106–33.
[11] Van der Geest 2002: 437–63; Mayneri 2016: 185–96; Ndlovu 2016: 29–39.

evangelistic imperative to encourage people to remain faithful to the Catholic church and to vindicate the Catholic church as the true church of Christ exercising spiritual authority. In the developing world, these challenges have created a tension between the Catholic hierarchy's duty to affirm Rome's generally cautious and reticent approach to matters concerning witchcraft on the one hand and the perceived pastoral importance of tackling a major dimension of people's spiritual (and indeed everyday) lives on the other.

Recent growth in the ministry of exorcism in the developed world, where exorcisms declined significantly in the aftermath of the Second Vatican Council, has meant a revival of demonology and, with it, a resurgence of interest in the reality and nature of witchcraft. Factors such as the influence of the Catholic Charismatic Renewal and the introduction of ideas from the developing world into the Catholicism of developed countries (through immigration and other means) have weakened the church's traditional hostility to engaging with belief in witchcraft, which has been a characteristic of official Catholicism since at least the eighteenth century. At the same time, however, evidence suggests that the church in the developing world is ill-equipped to deal pastorally with an intense fear of witchcraft that can spill over into violence and bloodshed.

2.2 Historic Catholic Attitudes to Witchcraft

Before the fourteenth century, ecclesiastical interest in harmful magic was largely confined to discrediting such beliefs and suppressing magic as a deluded form of undesirable superstition, an attitude most famously expressed in the tenth-century canon *Episcopi*.[12] It was not until the fourteenth century that theologians began to take an interest in the idea that the devil might be involved in witchcraft as something other than a mere deceiver, owing to development in the doctrine of the devil occasioned by the church's struggle against the Cathar heresy.[13] What followed was a steady 'diabolization' of magic and witchcraft, culminating in the notion that witches were a sect of devil worshippers who renounced their baptism and sacrificed children to Satan at their Sabbaths.[14]

Nevertheless, the idea of witches as devil-worshipping apostates remained a localized one in the late Middle Ages that never took hold in many nations. In Mediterranean Europe, for example, concern about the harmful potential of people believing in witchcraft continued to predominate over concern about witchcraft itself.[15] Medieval Catholicism thus produced both the myth of the witches' Sabbath and the intense witch persecutions in the fifteenth-century

---

[12] On the canon *Episcopi*, see Halsted 2020: 361–85.   [13] Baroja 1990: 19–43.
[14] Cameron 2010: 193–5.   [15] Baroja 1990: 40–2.

Rhine Valley on the one hand and a tradition of scepticism regarding the reality of witchcraft on the other. Those demonologists who believed most passionately that they were waging war against diabolical witchcraft emphasized the importance of the secular authorities' involvement in witchcraft prosecutions, with the inquisitor Heinrich Kramer (author of the notorious *Malleus Maleficarum*) arguing that the church's remedies were useless against witches in comparison with judicial punishment: 'the only possible way for [witchcraft] to be remedied is for the judges who are responsible for the sorceresses to get rid of them.'[16] The role of the church was to be the ideological engine of the war against witches, while the duty of the civil authorities was to extirpate them.

While Kramer's intention was to convince rulers and magistrates of the seriousness of the threat posed by witchcraft, by downplaying the role of the church, he made it possible for secular authorities to take charge of the prosecution of witchcraft in Protestant nations after the Reformation. Furthermore, Kramer weakened confidence in the church's sacraments, such as exorcism, as remedies against witchcraft.[17] On the other hand, others began to link the ancient idea of demonic possession with bewitchment,[18] with the consequence that exorcists and practical demonologists turned into experts on witchcraft. Towards the end of the sixteenth century, manuals of exorcism became increasingly preoccupied with witchcraft, to the point where exorcism merged with apotropaic counter-magical practices derived from popular religion.[19] By 1596, the Italian exorcist Girolamo Menghi was able to assert with confidence that all exorcists now accepted that most (if not all) cases of possession derived from witchcraft.[20] At the same time, however, the methodologies of the exorcists were increasingly alienated from those of inquisitors who (in Italy at least) were finding it harder to convict accused witches, with trials running on for years and ending in acquittals.[21]

As we shall see later in this Element, the tension between demonological experts and the ecclesiastical authorities would continue to be a theme in Catholic approaches to witchcraft. The eighteenth century saw the development of what Owen Davies has called a 'witchcraft without witches', where belief in and fear of bewitchment survived while the identification of specific individuals as culprits receded into the background – largely because neither secular nor ecclesiastical courts were willing to convict anyone for witchcraft.[22] From the late seventeenth century onwards, the concept of witchcraft became abstracted and depersonalized in demonological writings, and one reason for this was surely the withdrawal of judicial authorities from the detection and prosecution

---

[16] Institoris 2009: 413.   [17] Young 2016: 66.   [18] Midelfort 2005: 9.
[19] Young 2016: 110–11.   [20] Sluhovsky 2007: 85.   [21] Sluhovsky 2007: 81.
[22] Davies 1999: 280.

of accused witches. Indeed, in the eighteenth century, many jurisdictions switched their judicial focus from the prosecution of witches to the prosecution of vigilante action against supposed 'witches'.[23]

Far from being an 'Enlightenment' development prompted by secularization and opposed by the Catholic church, the eighteenth-century church supported and encouraged the decriminalization of witchcraft. In Poland–Lithuania, for example, bishops threatened to excommunicate anyone involved in the prosecution of witchcraft in the secular courts – not because Polish bishops did not believe in witchcraft but because they were determined to recover the church's sole right to try cases of witchcraft in the church courts.[24] Ironically, decriminalization of witchcraft became part of a conservative Catholic political agenda that sought to assert the church's authority over the state. The Spanish Inquisition, for example, was interested in witchcraft primarily as a superstitious imposture and executed no one for the crime throughout the seventeenth and eighteenth centuries.[25]

Throughout the eighteenth century, Catholic theologians increasingly argued that the power of the devil was more restricted than had hitherto been believed, retaining their allegiance to an orthodox belief in the existence of the devil and demons, and even the theoretical possibility of witchcraft, but restricting its field of operations. Theologians such as Ludovico Muratori, Scipione Maffei, and Ferdinand Sterzinger adopted a de facto scepticism regarding witchcraft that, even if it did not go so far as denying the possibility of its existence, eliminated witchcraft (to all practical intents and purposes) from the Catholic worldview.[26] While priests in rural areas continued to be involved in unbewitching in the nineteenth and twentieth centuries, and Catholic belief in witchcraft continued unabated in mission territories, the scepticism of the eighteenth century largely endured into the nineteenth and twentieth centuries among educated clergy.

2.3 Witchcraft and the Rise of 'Neo-Demonology'

As I outlined in *A History of Exorcism in Catholic Christianity*, it was Pope Leo XIII's encouragement of conspiracy theories involving Satanic elements at the end of the nineteenth century that was the proximate cause of a slow revival of practical demonology in the church, although this was initially focussed on a fear of politically motivated Satanism rather than on witchcraft.[27] However, an alternative anti-demonological strand also began to develop in Catholic theology that gained traction in the church in the aftermath of the Second

---

[23] Young forthcoming.　　[24] Ostling 2011: 55–6.　　[25] Lehner 2016: 136.
[26] Lehner 2016: 143–51.　　[27] Young 2016: 184–91.

Vatican Council in the 1960s and 1970s. Theologians questioned the scriptural and doctrinal foundations of belief in the demonic realm and all that it entailed, and by the 1970s, even the existence of the devil as a personal being seemed to be in question in Catholic theology.[28] Jesuit theologians such as Herbert Haag, Henry Ansgar Kelly, and Juan B. Cortés led the attack on traditional belief in the devil, which became so serious that Pope Paul VI felt compelled to respond in 1972 with a reiteration of the church's traditional teaching on the existence of Satan as an evil personal being.[29]

However, while these theologians' willingness to question the *existence* of Satan and demons was new, there was nothing new about Catholic theologians exercising extreme caution when it came to 'interference ... by malignant agencies at the request of man'.[30] In a 1915 dissertation on the subject, the Notre Dame Sister Antoinette Marie Pratt dismissed the witch trials as the product of hysteria and excessive imagination, echoing much the same explanations then offered by secular historians. The attitude of the Jesuit theologian Christiano Pesch, writing at the very end of the nineteenth century, reflected a general disengagement of Catholic theologians from the issue of witchcraft that continued into the twentieth century:

> *A priori* we ought to be very slow in admitting in a given case that diabolical influence exists unless it is proved by irrefutable arguments. In matters of this kind, the greatest incredulity is preferable to credulity, when there is question of men who make a business of such things. On the other hand, not all the narrations about compacts with demons are simply to be rejected as fables .... But in passing such judgements, the greatest caution is required, because in things so remote from the senses mistakes are very easily made.[31]

In addition to condoning almost unlimited scepticism with regard to witchcraft, it is noteworthy that Pesch worked on the assumption that judgements about the reality of demonic pacts would largely be a historical exercise. It should come as no surprise that the clergy of the post–Vatican II era found it easy to disbelieve in witchcraft; such disbelief was already rooted in an earlier theology that, while paying lip service to demonology, had to all intents and purposes abandoned its practical implications.

The Catholic clergy's cautious approach to claims of witchcraft and Satanism in the early 1970s is exemplified by their response to an apparent outbreak of 'black magic' in the north of Ireland, then riven by sectarian armed conflict, during 1973–1974. While rumours of occult rituals may have been fanned (or even started) by the British army in an effort to keep people in their homes after

---

[28] Giordan and Possamai 2018: 42–6.   [29] Young 2016: 213–15.   [30] Pratt 1915: 118.
[31] Pesch 1898: iii, 445.

dark, Catholic priests tended to confine themselves to denouncing 'dabbling' in the occult from the pulpit and distributing holy water.[32] It is possible that priests blessed some of those houses in which the paraphernalia of occult rituals were allegedly found, as children interviewed at the time referred to priests blessing houses.[33] However, one priest interviewed by a local newspaper attributed people's dabbling with the occult through the use of Ouija boards as a result of boredom and wearily observed that 'If [black magic] practices are going on, we would probably be the last to know about them.'[34] Certainly, there was little sign that rumours of 'black magic' in the north of Ireland produced moral panic in the Catholic clergy, who surely had many more pressing pastoral problems to deal with.

For those theologians sceptical of the very existence of a personal devil, the question of the existence of witchcraft scarcely arose. However, a highly publicized exorcism in Germany during 1975–1976 brought the supposed role of witchcraft in demonic possession back to public attention. In September 1975, the bishop of Würzburg authorized the exorcism of a young woman named Anneliese Michel, who underwent months of exorcism before dying of malnutrition (while still being exorcized) in July 1976. The resulting criminal case against the exorcists resulted in their extensive notes and recordings (usually kept secret) becoming public. One of the exorcists, Arnold Renz, recorded a conversation with the 'demon' allegedly possessing Michel that revealed the reason for her possession was witchcraft:

> It is the village that lives and breathes in the answer to the question of why Anneliese was being possessed. [The demon said] 'She was not born yet when she was cursed.' A woman had done it out of envy. Who was she? 'A neighbor of her mother's in Leiblfing.' Did she also curse others? Obstinate silence . . . Anneliese's parents tried to check the story out, but the woman had died.[35]

As the exorcisms went on, however, the idea of witchcraft receded into the background as the exorcists began to believe the possession was first and foremost a trial sent by God to test the saintly Anneliese.[36] Nevertheless, the case demonstrated that belief in witchcraft as a cause of the demonic attack was not only very much alive in rural Catholic Bavaria, but exorcists were also still prepared to entertain the possibility of such things.

Perhaps partly as a result of the fallout from the death of Anneliese Michel, willingness to deal with the problem of witchcraft was at a low ebb in the church in parts of western Europe in the 1970s. For example, by the early 1980s,

---

[32] Jenkins 2014: 209.   [33] Jenkins 2014: 176.   [34] Jenkins 2014: 211.
[35] Goodman 2005: 97–8.   [36] Young 2016: 216–19.

Belgian monks who had long been the last resort of rural people who believed themselves to be the victims of witchcraft often had to be tricked into 'unwitching' people. The monks found themselves walking a tightrope between retaining the trust of local people and reinforcing beliefs they considered superstitious. Since the monks were increasingly reluctant to distribute the blessed salt, holy water, and medals that had once warded off witchcraft, people began to resort to the parish clergy they considered less powerful. However, the monks could still sometimes be induced to give a blessing that was then construed as an 'unwitching' by its recipients.[37] In her research in the bocage in the 1970s, Jeanne Favret-Saada found that the diocesan exorcist had been appointed specifically *because* he was sceptical of peasant belief in witchcraft.[38] The exorcist made a sharp distinction between witchcraft (which was superstition) and demonic possession (which might be genuine).[39]

In comparison with the cultural influence of the book and film, *The Exorcist*, the latter of which was released in 1973, the real-world exorcism of Anneliese Michel was a rather insignificant event. The central role played by the awakening of an ancient curse in the plot of *The Exorcist* strengthened the popular perception of a link between curses and demonic possession (in contrast to the traditional link between possession and sin emphasized by the church over centuries), and the novel and film may also have influenced exorcists and demonologists themselves.[40] The cultural influence of *The Exorcist* represented the beginning of what might be termed a 'neo-demonological' Catholic backlash against the demonological scepticism of post-conciliar theologians like Haag.

The 'neo-demonology' that first emerged in the 1970s and 1980s differed from the traditional demonology that preceded it in its relative absence of sceptical caution and in its willingness to draw on non-Catholic theological sources, most notably Pentecostalism (through the Catholic Charismatic Renewal). While the abandonment of the demonological reticence that characterized much Catholic theological writing in the eighteenth and nineteenth centuries was begun by Pope Leo XIII at the end of the nineteenth century, it intensified in the 1980s as a result of the emergence of the 'Satanic Abuse Panic' in the United States. Psychiatrists noticed that children undergoing treatment claimed to 'remember' horrific Satanic rituals in which they had been abused by family members and communities. The idea soon spread to Europe, where the testimony of supposed survivors of Satanic Ritual Abuse was used to bring convictions that were later deemed unsound, on the grounds that psychiatrists

---

[37] De Blécourt 1999: 185–6.   [38] Favret-Saada 1977: 18.   [39] Favret-Saada 1977: 127.
[40] Young 2016: 219.

used leading methods of questioning and it was possible for children to form false memories.[41]

Jean La Fontaine has observed that the mythology of Satanic Ritual Abuse had a particularly Protestant character and was rooted in the English-speaking world and countries where English was commonly spoken as a second language. Most Catholic countries seemed 'relatively immune' to the mythology, with France remaining virtually untouched by the phenomenon.[42] Even in the United States, where the mythology of Satanic Ritual Abuse originated, Catholic exorcists are reticent in giving credence to the full range of claims made about it, even if they are prepared to use the term. Vincent Lampert, for example, includes a section on 'Satanic Ritual Abuse' in his book on exorcism but does not go into any detail about it and mentions only the dedication of children to Satan at birth.[43] The mythology's failure to take root in France, in spite of France's rich tradition of tales of sacrilegious diabolism, is curious – and indeed, it is possible that France's native traditions concerning Satanism rendered the importation of an American cultural phenomenon surplus to requirements.

Yet while the specifics of Satanic Ritual Abuse mythology failed to appeal to Catholic demonologists to the same extent as their Protestant counterparts, the accusations confirmed the general idea that people were actively engaged in Satanic worship – a key element of the witchcraft myth of late medieval and early modern demonologists. Whereas belief in demon-worshipping sorcerers had been confined in the mid-twentieth century to fringe eccentrics such as Montague Summers, by the end of the century, a link between witchcraft, curses, and Satanic worship was once more being promoted by Catholic exorcists. The emergence of the Catholic Charismatic Renewal from the late 1960s onwards, which incorporated some elements of a Pentecostal theology of spiritual healing into Catholic theology and practice, served not only to normalize exorcism but also helped to make the possibility of witchcraft seem like a reasonable proposition to some theologians.

Charismatic theology emphasizes the reality of Satanic opposition to the Holy Spirit, while witchcraft appears largely in the idea of spiritual bondage as an ancestral curse (or a curse derived from events in a person's childhood, perhaps including Satanic Ritual Abuse).[44] The legitimacy of the Charismatic Renewal as a strand within post-conciliar Catholic spirituality was greatly strengthened by the publication of *Renewal and the Powers of Darkness* by the Belgian Cardinal Léon-Joseph Suenens in 1983,[45] with a foreword by

---

[41] La Fontaine 1999: 115–38; Frankfurter 2008: 2–3.   [42] La Fontaine 1999: 132.
[43] Lampert 2020: 91–2.   [44] Walker 1993: 86–97.   [45] Suenens 1983.

Cardinal Joseph Ratzinger (the future Pope Benedict XVI). However, the contribution of Suenens and Ratzinger was also intended as a corrective of some of the perceived excesses of the Renewal, and the Congregation for the Doctrine of the Faith (led by Ratzinger) later condemned the practice of laypeople making use of 'minor exorcisms', which sometimes occurred in charismatic gatherings.[46]

In recent years, the 'Satanic Panic' appears to have returned in the form of the so-called QAnon conspiracy theory in the United States, which alleges the existence of a 'deep state' conspiracy to cover up child abuse by high-ranking figures and often draws on the mythology of Satanic Ritual Abuse. On 28 October 2020, Archbishop Carlo Maria Viganò, a former Papal Nuncio to the United States who is a vocal proponent of conspiracy theories in support of former US president Donald Trump, signalled his commitment to the same ideas as the QAnon conspiracy theorists in an interview with BardsFM, including the idea that a malevolent global elite was involved in witchcraft:

> The enemy, in reality, is no longer invisible. The web of corruption, pedo-philia, child pornography, ritual homicides, and Satanic worship unites all – and I repeat, all – of these servants of the global elite. Even those who pursue only economic interests, in the end, know that their bosses in one way or another are involved in criminal trafficking and are friends with people linked to the occult and witchcraft – think of Marina Abramovic, for example – who in turn are celebrity endorsers of Bill Gates and the Rothschilds, are invited to parties with the Clintons and John Podesta, with the Obamas, or to Epstein's island.[47]

While Viganò is a fringe figure, a number of US clergy have been outspoken proponents of political conspiracy theories and are often willing to make use of demonological language and even make use of the exorcism of Pope Leo XIII.[48] Indeed, the cultural roots of this kind of Catholic conspiracism are to be found in Leo XIII's political paranoia about Freemasons and Satanists, and while it may result in accusations of Satanism and witchcraft being hurled at public figures, there are no obvious signs that it is breeding increased fear of witchcraft in the conventional sense of particular threats of supernatural harm. Furthermore, clerical involvement in conspiracy theories associated with the far-right is confined to the United States and is probably attributable to the United States's very specific political and cultural conditions. Viganò remains an isolated figure in his endorsement of the QAnon conspiracy theory.

---

[46] Young 2016: 224–9.   [47] Viganò 2020.   [48] Winters 2020.

3 Witchcraft in Modern Vatican Documents

The highest level of the modern church's 'official' attitude to witchcraft is embodied in four documents, two liturgical and two catechetical: the rubrics of the Tridentine rite of exorcism of 1614 (which remained the sole rite of exorcism until 1999 and received renewed authorization in 2011), the *Praenotanda* to the new rite of exorcism promulgated during 1998–1999, the teaching document *Christian Faith and Demonology* (1975), and *The Catechism of the Catholic Church* (1992).[49]

3.1 Witchcraft in the Tridentine Rite of Exorcism (1614)

The rite of exorcism was the last part of the liturgy to be revised after the Council of Trent; it was also the liturgy that remained in force, unamended, for the longest period after the Second Vatican Council. The Tridentine rite found in the *Rituale Romanum*, sometimes known by its formal title *De exorcizandis obsessis a demonio* (*DEOD*, 'Of the exorcism of those obsessed by a demon'), was thus the authorized rite of exorcism at the time when many current diocesan exorcists were appointed and trained, and understanding it is critical to appreciating responses to witchcraft in the contemporary church. Furthermore, since 2011, the 1614 rite of exorcism has been authorized by the pontifical commission *Ecclesia Dei* under the norms governing the 'extraordinary form' of the liturgy (the Tridentine liturgy in use before 1962).

The revision of the rite of exorcism began as early as 1584, when Pope Gregory XIII instructed Cardinal Giulio Antonio Santori to create a rite of exorcism for the universal church to replace the many local variations that had grown over the decades. Instead of drawing on the vaunted expertise of the celebrated exorcists of his own era (such as Girolamo Menghi), Santori's antiquarian instinct bypassed the late sixteenth-century exorcism industry and returned to the texts of eighth-century pontificals, while he relied on the *Liber sacerdotalis* ('priest's book') of Alberto da Castello (1523) for commentary.[50]

Castello was by no means dismissive of witchcraft, which Santori included alongside despair, sin, and the salvation of souls as one of the four reasons for demonic possession, but his reliance on an earlier author meant that Santori ignored the excessive demonological preoccupation with witchcraft that marked authors like Menghi. Although Santori's rite of exorcism and commentary were never formally adopted, they formed the basis for the rite authorized by Pope Paul V in 1614.[51] Witchcraft is mentioned twice in the rubrics of the 1614 rite, first in guidance on interpreting the dreams of demoniacs:

---

[49] Congregation for the Doctrine of the Faith 1975; John Paul II 1992.
[50] Sluhovsky 2007: 87. [51] Sluhovsky 2007: 88.

> Other [dreams] reveal witchcraft committed (*factum maleficium*), and by whom it was committed, and the way to dispel it. But let [the exorcist] beware lest [the demoniac] fly to magicians or to witches (*sagas*) or to others, rather than to the ministers of the church; or lest any superstition or other illicit way is used. For when the devil calms the sick person, and permits them to receive the holy Eucharist, it may seem as if he has left. Finally, the arts and frauds of the devil for deceiving men are innumerable; the exorcist ought to be cautious lest he err.[52]

The dominant note in this instruction is caution on the part of the exorcist, and it is noticeable that this rubric does not actually endorse the reality of witchcraft as a cause of possession. The rubric's principal concerns are that the demoniac should not seek the assistance of witches (perhaps an allusion to the idea that only a witch could undo what they had inflicted) and that the devil is deceitful.

Further on in the rubrics, the rite is less non-committal about witchcraft, however. In instructions on what the exorcist may or may not say to a demoniac, the exorcist is advised that

He may command the demon to say whether it is detained in that body on account of some work of magic (*operam magicam*) or sign or instrument of witchcraft (*malefica signa, vel instrumenta*) which, if the obsessed person has taken by mouth, they may vomit up; or if they were elsewhere outside the body, that [the demon] should reveal them; and let them be burnt once they are revealed.[53]

This doctrine of *maleficalia* (instruments of witchcraft), while presented here very concisely, is much the same as what was to be found in contemporary manuals of exorcism. In conjunction with the provision that the exorcist might ask 'how [demons] have entered, [and] concerning the cause' (*quo ingressi sunt, de causa*),[54] the 1614 rite of exorcism gives a great deal of latitude to the exploration of witchcraft as a potential cause of possession.

On the other hand, while the 1614 rite refers to the detection of witchcraft, it makes no mention whatsoever of the detection of witches, with witches (*sagas*) appearing in the rubrics only as a set of people to be avoided. The 1614 rite thus appears to rule out the sort of probative exorcisms practised by some exorcists at the time, and within a century the rubrics of the rite would come to underpin an eighteenth-century campaign by the Roman Inquisition against *all* alternative rites and manuals of exorcism.[55] Initially, however, Rome's Sacred Congregation of Rites did not attempt to suppress local rites authorized by the bishop, presenting the 1614 liturgy as guidelines. Yet, as Moshe Sluhovsky has argued, by promising efficacy and turning exorcism into a de facto sacrament

---

[52] *DEOD*: 199/207 (§§ 867–8).   [53] *DEOD*: 200/208 (§ 879).   [54] *DEOD*: 200/208 (§ 874).
[55] Young 2016: 162–5.

(as opposed to the rather trivial sacramental of the Middle Ages), the 1614 liturgy established a trajectory that ended in the suppression of all other manuals of exorcism.[56]

3.2 The Significance of *Christian Faith and Demonology* (1975)

The post-conciliar teaching document *Christian Faith and Demonology* (*CFD*) was first published in the Vatican newspaper *L'Osservatore Romano* on 26 June 1975 as an official statement of the Congregation for the Doctrine of the Faith on the subject of demonology, which was a theologically contested issue at the time owing to the writings of revisionist theologians like Herbert Haag.[57] While the primary focus of *CFD* was the theologically fundamental question of whether Satan existed as a personal being (unsurprisingly, the Vatican document affirmed traditional teaching), the document also dwelt on the subject of superstition. Indeed, the document opened with a reminder of the church's historic condemnation of superstition: 'The many forms of superstition, obsessional preoccupation with Satan and the demons, and the different kinds of worship of them or attachment to them have always been condemned by the Church.'

The document insisted that 'Christian teaching . . . has forbidden superstition just as much as magic', and cited 'the Mosaic Law' (presumably a reference to the First Commandment 'You shall have no other gods before me' (Exodus 20:2/Deuteronomy 5:6)) as well as Exodus 22:18, Leviticus 19:26, Leviticus 19:31, Leviticus 20:27, and Deuteronomy 18:10–11 as condemnations of magic, astrology, necromancy, divination, the calling up of spirits and 'soothsayers, astrologers, magicians, sorcerers, charmers, those who summoned up ghosts or spirits and those who consulted the dead'. The document went on to cite condemnations of magical practices by ecclesiastical synods and councils.

While *CFD* was not directly focussed on witchcraft, the document emerged from an era when the church was on the defensive with regard to demonology, and it displays a certain anxiety regarding superstition and any perception that the church might indulge in. The reiteration of traditional condemnations of magical practices is therefore balanced by a rejection of 'superstition' even if no definition of superstition is offered other than 'obsessional preoccupation with Satan and the demons'. It is a stretch to interpret this as a condemnation of belief in witchcraft, although it is possible that *CFD*'s anxiety about unhealthy preoccupation with demonic activity was one inspiration for the cautious *Praenotanda* of the 1999 rite of exorcism.

---

[56] Sluhovsky 2007: 91–3.   [57] Congregation for the Doctrine of the Faith 1975: 6–10.

3.3 Witchcraft in *The Catechism of the Catholic Church* (1992)

The Catechism of the Catholic Church (*CCC*) was promulgated by Pope John Paul II on 7 December 1992 as a single document for the faithful setting out the totality of the church's teaching on faith and morals.[58] The *Catechism*'s teaching on divination and magic[59] forms part of the teaching on the First Commandment. While *CCC* §2116 concerns divination, *CCC* §2117 deals with *magia* and *veneficium*, offering a definition of magic and sorcery as an attempt to dominate occult powers, including practices intended to restore health. The text implies that not all magic will involve the intention of harming someone or seeking the aid of demons and condemns the wearing of *amuleta* (a word covering both charms and amulets). The section also condemns Spiritualism and, without condemning them outright, warns that traditional cures should not involve recourse to demons:

> All practices of magic (*magiae*) or sorcery (*veneficii*), by which one attempts to tame occult powers (*occultas vires dominari*), so as to place them at one's service and have a supernatural power over others – even if this were for the sake of restoring their health – are gravely contrary to the virtue of religion. These practices are even more to be condemned when accompanied by the intention of harming someone, or when they have recourse to the intervention of demons. Wearing charms (*amuleta*) is also reprehensible. Spiritism often implies divination or magical practices; the Church for her part warns the faithful against it. Recourse to so-called traditional cures does not justify either the invocation of evil powers or the exploitation of another's credulity.[60]

CCC §2117 echoes the traditional language of pontificals and articles of visitation stretching back many centuries, but it is noteworthy that the *Catechism* offers no account whatsoever of the mechanism by which magic or sorcery might work. Indeed, it is possible to read the text from a sceptical position that denies the reality or effectiveness of witchcraft, since it condemns 'attempts' at taming occult powers, the 'intention' of harming someone by occult means, 'recourse to the intervention of demons' (without saying that demons really do intervene on a witch's behalf), and 'the invocation of evil powers' (without saying whether such an invocation might work).

It may seem tendentious to interpret *CCC* §2117 as consistent with unbelief in witchcraft. However, in the context of longstanding ecclesiastical

---

[58] Ratzinger 1994: 9–36.   [59] *CCC*: §§2115–17.

[60] For the Latin text see www.vatican.va/archive/catechism_lt/p3s2c1a1_lt.htm#III.%20%C2%AB%20Non%20habebis%20deos%20alienos%20coram%20me%20%C2%BB, accessed 8 May 2021. For the official English text see www.vatican.va/archive/ENG0015/__P7E.HTM, accessed 8 May 2021.

condemnations of occult practices by bishops who did not believe in the reality of the power of witches, this interpretation is not only valid but was perhaps even intended by the authors of the *Catechism*. The text is certainly not a clear endorsement of the reality of any of the powers claimed by magic or witchcraft, and the impiety of *attempting* to recruit the aid of demons remains a grave sin even if it is impossible for magicians to do this. On the other hand, it is easy for those already convinced of the reality of magic and witchcraft to read *CCC* §2117 as an endorsement of their beliefs. It is a section of the *Catechism* that is best read and understood in the long tradition of canonical prohibitions on involvement in the occult arts rather than as an official statement of demonology; it is far too thin to be the latter.

3.4 Witchcraft in the Revised Rite of Exorcism (1999)

The rite of exorcism was the last part of the church's liturgy to be revised following the Second Vatican Council (1962–1965); it was announced on 22 November 1998 and finally published (in Latin) on 26 January 1999 as *De exorcismis supplicationibus quibusdam* (*DESQ*, 'Of exorcisms and certain supplications'), by which time the 1614 rite of exorcism had been in use for 385 years.[61] The rubrics of the 1614 rite were replaced (or, on another interpretation, supplemented) by a series of *Praenotanda* governing the conduct of exorcism. Whereas the 1614 rite affirmed (or at least heavily implied) the reality of witchcraft, the 1999 *Praenotanda* offered an apparent rejection of it. As *Praenotandum* 15 declares,

> Let [the exorcist] rightly distinguish cases of diabolical attack from that false opinion whereby some people, even the faithful, think themselves to be an object of witchcraft (*maleficii*), of bad luck (*malae sortis*), or a curse (*maledictionis*), which are cast by others upon them, or upon those close to them, or upon their goods.[62]

While it is possible to read *Praenotandum* 15 as a rejection of belief in witchcraft, the focus of the *Praenotandum* is not in fact belief in the possibility of witchcraft, bad luck, and curses in and of itself. The *Praenotandum* does not condemn such belief, but rather people's belief that they are *afflicted* by witchcraft, bad luck, and curses. On an even more restrictive reading, the *Praenotandum* condemns only the belief that someone is afflicted by curses cast on them by others, as a disincentive to accusations of witchcraft.

The careful phrasing of the *Praenotandum* to allow such interpretations is consistent with the measured scepticism adopted by the church over the last

---

[61] Young 2016: 231.   [62] *DESQ*: 11–12.

three centuries in which hesitancy about accepting the possibility of witchcraft
as a mechanism of demonic vexation was coupled with consistent affirmation of
the reality of the demonic itself. In addition to identifying the belief that one is
the victim of witchcraft, bad luck, or a curse as a 'false opinion', *Praenotandum*
15 also forbids the exorcism of those who believe themselves to be victims of
witchcraft:

> [The exorcist] should not deny them spiritual help, but let him not allow
> exorcism. He may, in fact, offer other suitable prayers, with them and for
> them, so that they may find the peace of God. Likewise, spiritual help should
> not be refused to believers, whom the Evil One does not touch (cf. 1 John
> 5:18), but who are badly tried by him when they want to preserve their fidelity
> to the Lord Jesus and to the Gospel. This can also be done by a priest who is
> not an exorcist, or even by a deacon, with suitable and permitted prayers and
> supplications.

In quoting 1 John 5:18, 'We know that anyone born of God does not sin, but
He who was born of God keeps him, and the evil one does not touch him', the
Praenotandum appears to stray into theology. If it is not possible for the devil to
'touch' believers, even though he may try or tempt them, this may imply that the
devil cannot infest, obsess, or possess faithful Catholics – unless, perhaps, they
give in to temptation. *Praenotandum* 15 heavily implies that the right way to
deal with someone who believes themselves to be the victim of bad luck or
a curse cast by another person is to attempt to convince them otherwise. This
aspect of the *Praenotanda* has received insufficient attention, since it undermines the basic theological rationale of belief in witchcraft as an explanation for
the demonic affliction of the innocent. If such a thing is not possible – following
Praenotandum 15's interpretation of 1 John 5:18 – then the witchcraft hypothesis is essentially unnecessary.

In addition to *Praenotandum* 15, *Praenotandum* 19 instructs that 'Exorcism
is to be carried out in such a way that it manifests the faith of the Church and no-
one can consider it a magical or superstitious act (*actio magica vel
superstitiosa*).'[63] In this way, there should be no possibility of confusion
between the ministry of the exorcist and the services offered by occultists or
folk magical practitioners. However, the *Praenotanda* give some latitude to
national bishops' conferences in their implementation of the rite of exorcism in
any given territory, permitting variation of the 'signs and actions' (*signa et
gesta*) of the rites 'with regard to the culture and distinctiveness of a people'
(*attenta cultura et genio . . . populi*). They also allow bishops' conferences to
add a pastoral directory on the use of major exorcism.[64] Bishops' conferences

---

[63] *DESQ*: 12.   [64] *DESQ*: 15–16.

were also authorized to produce official translations of the rite of exorcism, which has naturally permitted a degree of interpretation of the Latin text. While the English translation did not appear until 2017, an Italian translation existed from as early as 2004. Rather than literally translating the phrase *falsa opinione*, the Italian version of the rite glossed it as *credulità* (credulity) – a choice that significantly weakened the force of *Praenotandum* 15's warning against a 'false opinion' regarding witchcraft.[65]

3.4.1 Current Status of the 1614 Rite of Exorcism's Instructions on Witchcraft in Relation to the 1999 Praenotanda

On 30 April 2011, Cardinal William Levada, president of the pontifical commission *Ecclesia Dei*, issued a clarification on the implementation of Pope Benedict XVI's apostolic letter *Summorum Pontificum* (2007), which permitted general use of the Tridentine liturgy predating 1962 (the 'extraordinary form' of the liturgy). One of the clarifications in this document was that the use of the Tridentine *Rituale Romanum* was permitted in contexts where the 'extraordinary form' was customarily used.[66] Francesco Bamonte, president of the International Association of Exorcists, then wrote to the pontifical commission *Ecclesia Dei* on 21 June 2011 seeking further clarification regarding the permissibility of the 1614 rite of exorcism. Guido Pozzo, the commission's secretary general, confirmed that use of the 1614 rite was authorized under the terms of Cardinal Levada's clarification of 30 April,[67] thus opening the way to the use of both rites by exorcists.

Pozzo did not clarify whether the re-authorization of the rite of 1614 implied the authorization of its rubrics as well – especially where, as in their approach to witchcraft, they apparently differ from the 1999 *Praenotanda*. However, if we presume that the *Praenotanda* have the force of canon law, under the principle that alterations of canon do not abrogate a previous law unless the new canon expressly indicates it, is directly contrary to it, or 'reorganizes the whole matter of the previous law in its entirety',[68] it is reasonable to suppose that the rubrics of the 1614 rite do apply, at least when that rite is used by an exorcist. Bamonte's approach to the canonical status of the issue of witchcraft, writing before the re-authorization of the 1614 rite, was a nuanced one:

> The subject of witchcraft is one of the most delicate for us exorcists, because it easily lends itself to the risk of generating psychosis: therefore, we understand the legitimate concern of those who have prepared the new rite of exorcisms. The editors of that text, while not at all excluding the concrete possibility that sometimes the curse is actually and effectively implemented,

---

[65] Nanni 2004: 246.   [66] Levada and Pozzo 2011.   [67] *Ecclesia Dei* 2012: 9.   [68] *CDC*: 20.

as clearly stated in the *Rituale Romanum* in n. 8 and no. 20 of the *Normae observandae circa exorcizandos a daemonio*, in my opinion want to avoid the risk of attributing any difficulty or negative event to a curse performed by someone against us. In fact, even if it cannot be denied that sometimes a curse is actually carried out against someone, nevertheless we must not favour the mentality according to which the curse, whether real or presumed, becomes a convenient excuse for not assuming one's responsibilities.[69]

Clearly, even before the re-authorization of the rite in 2011, Bamonte considered that the rubrics of the 1614 rite of exorcism remained binding on the exorcist and interpreted *Praenotandum* 15 as primarily pastoral in intent. The 'mentality' that attributes misfortunes to curses laid by others, as a means of evading 'moral responsibility' is at fault. Like the Italian translation of the 1999 rite, which preferred 'credulity' to 'false opinion' when characterizing belief in witchcraft, Bamonte treated the *Praenotanda* as a shift in emphasis towards caution rather than a theological statement that challenged the 'witchcraft hypothesis'.

At the time of writing, the impact on exorcism of Pope Francis's apostolic letter *Traditionis custodes* (2021), which placed numerous restrictions on the extraordinary form of the Roman rite, remains unclear. However, since the apostolic letter handed authority over the use of the extraordinary form back to bishops, it seems likely that bishops will have the authority to forbid the use of the 1614 rite of exorcism in their dioceses.

4 Witchcraft and the Exorcists

This section will examine in detail the writings of five exorcists on the subject of witchcraft, all of them at one time authorized to act as exorcists in European or North American dioceses. Since the 1990s – largely following the lead of Fr Gabriele Amorth – Catholic exorcists have been increasingly public and vocal about their ministry, while their writings have been eagerly consumed by a general public intrigued by the subject of exorcism. Since exorcists are often the first port of call for Catholics who believe themselves to be bewitched, it is exorcists who usually consider themselves to be experts on the subject of witchcraft, taking it upon themselves to interpret the norms of the 1614 and 1999 rites of exorcism in the light of their own experience. Exorcists' approaches to witchcraft are therefore informed not only by the official documents of the church but also by their specific cultural context and the approach to witchcraft generally adopted within their bishops' conference.

---

[69] Bamonte 2006: 215.

There has been little quantitative research into exorcists, but in 2015 Giuseppe Giordan and Adam Possamai surveyed the clergy of one southern European Catholic diocese with a large number of priests (over 500) and found that, while priests between 60 and 75 years old often did not regard the devil as a real person, priests between 45 and 60 did not usually deny the devil's existence but commonly expressed uncertainty about his nature. However, priests between 30 and 45 were clear that the devil really existed and that he could take possession of human beings.[70] The researchers were unsurprised by the generational fracture in clerical attitudes to the devil, attributing it to the influence of the post-conciliar atmosphere of disenchantment on older priests, while the vocations of younger clergy emerged out of a resurgence of traditional Catholic orthodoxy that may be particularly associated with the pontificate of Benedict XVI (2005–2013).

Some quantitative research on the significance of witchcraft in the ministry of an exorcist was carried out in 2015 by Giordan and Possamai, who obtained an electronic spreadsheet from an exorcist in southern Europe detailing his consultations over a ten-year period. Giordan and Possamai found that 17.4 per cent of cases dealt with by the exorcist involved 'evil influences', defined as 'Suspicion of knowledge of being affected by evil influences, the evil eye, evil spells or curses' (these were features of a total of 187 cases). A slightly higher percentage of cases (19.1 per cent) involved 'Occultism and Satanism', defined very broadly by the exorcist as 'Involvement with occult arts, alternative spiritualities, Satanic sects and rituals, folk/alternative healing practices, and also masonry.'[71]

While these proportions may seem low, of those cases that actually resulted in an exorcism being performed, 51 per cent (28 of 55) involved suspicions of the evil eye and spells. The exorcist's questioning was then focussed on 'trying to pinpoint precisely who in the family or entourage of friends may have cast the evil eye or curse, or has been the medium of a possible demonic possession'.[72] In 20 per cent of cases, the exorcist or the sufferer was able to identify 'the presence of a person, usually a woman, renowned as a witch, medium, or sorceress, who had thrown an evil eye or participated in Voodoo or Wicca rituals'. For example, a forty-two-year-old woman known as 'C' who was 'an established lawyer' contacted the exorcist because she believed she was being targeted by her sister-in-law, who had joined an 'esoteric sect'. Under exorcism, 'C' admitted to having belonged to an occult secret society in the past and began vomiting animal skin, hair, sticks, bones, and dust – an

[70] Giordan and Possamai 2018: 61–2.   [71] Giordan and Possamai 2018: 55
[72] Giordan and Possamai 2018: 72–3.

apparent case of the ingested *maleficalia* mentioned in the rubrics of the 1614 rite of exorcism.

The exorcist's desire to trace demonic influence to its root cause often results in the possibility of witchcraft being raised, even implicitly, to account for preternatural phenomena. This can be seen in North America as well as Europe. In a 2012 report prepared for the bishop of Gary, Indiana in the United States, Fr Michael Maginot recorded the discovery of 'many disturbing things' in soil beneath the house of Latoya Ammons (whose son had allegedly been witnessed walking backwards up a wall), implying that the objects were in some way *maleficalia* and causes of the phenomena. Bishop Dale Melczek authorized the exorcism of Latoya Ammons's son on 30 May 2012.[73]

One interpretation of the prominence of witchcraft as a diagnosed cause of demonic vexation in those exorcized – in contrast to the fairly small role played by witchcraft in the totality of all cases dealt with by an exorcist – is that where the exorcist's questioning revealed the possibility of witchcraft, he was more willing to exorcize. If this is true, then understanding belief in witchcraft may be key to understanding the resurgence of exorcism in the contemporary Catholic church. Giordan and Possamai's approach, in which witchcraft 'does not seem to be relevant in late modernity' and was therefore excluded from their analysis, does not seem helpful.[74] On the contrary, the evidence points to belief in witchcraft and curses playing a significant role in requests for exorcism in Italy, the country where exorcists are most willing to write about their ministry. While the strength of belief in witchcraft in Italy may not be typical of western Europe, it may well be more typical of Catholic countries worldwide. In 1995, the bishops' conference of Tuscany in north-central Italy was sufficiently concerned about the problem of witchcraft to produce a pastoral note on the subject:

> Some of the faithful ask themselves: is the 'hex' (*fattura*) true? Does it have any real effects? Can the devil use bad people and therefore gestures such as the 'hex' or the 'evil eye' to harm someone? The answer is certainly difficult for individual cases, but it is not possible to exclude, in practices of this kind, some participation of the act of witchcraft (*gesto malefico*) in the demonic world, and vice versa. For this reason the Church has always firmly rejected and rejects *maleficium* and any action related to it.[75]

Clearly, the church's firm rejection of witchcraft in this case was not a rejection of belief in witchcraft, but a rejection of witchcraft itself and, by

---

[73] Laycock 2020: 286–7.   [74] Giordan and Possamai 2018: 35.
[75] Conferenza episcopale della Toscana 1995.

implication, any magical practices of counter-witchcraft ('any action related to it').

In contrast to Italy, witchcraft is of relatively minor significance in the equally Catholic European nation of Poland. For the Polish exorcists Andrzej Grefkowicz (exorcist of the archdiocese of Warsaw), Marian Piątkowski (exorcist of the archdiocese of Poznán), and Slawomir Sosnowski (exorcist of the archdiocese of Łodz), witchcraft and spells (*czary, zaklęcia*) do not play a major role in their demonology, but they do provide a means of explaining why religious and devout people who avoid any contact with suspect spiritualities sometimes experience demonic interference. The exorcists suggest that, where there are intergenerational spiritual problems, 'perhaps someone in the family cast witchcraft or spells',[76] and they acknowledge the possibility of 'bad intentions' (*zle intencje*) causing evil alongside spells and curses (*złorzeczy*).[77]

The French bishops have historically adopted a very cautious approach to exorcism and demonology,[78] but they have also adopted a policy of dealing publicly with the subject rather than hiding it from view. In 2017, the French bishops' conference's *Service National de la Pastorale Liturgique et Sacramentelle* (National Pastoral Liturgy and Sacramental Service) collaborated with the *Bureau National des Exorcistes* (National Bureau of Exorcists) to produce a guide to exorcism that dealt briefly with the issue of those who come to the exorcist concerned about witchcraft:

> Certain persons wish to be protected from evil influences, that is to say those caused by witchcraft (*maléfiques*). The minister who receives this kind of request will be sure to disengage it from false impressions and will put in evidence the dignity of the subject, appealing to their freedom in the faith and their sense of responsibility.[79]

Witchcraft also features prominently in the French bishops' introduction to exorcism on the website of the Catholic church in France, which explains that 'The exorcist's mission is to welcome suffering people who think they are victims of witchcraft (*maléfices*) or feel under the influence of the devil; he listens to them and discerns with them the origin of their discomfort, prays with them and on them and in the case of possession celebrates an exorcism.'[80] In both cases, the French bishops suggest that witchcraft (if that is how *maléfices* should be translated, rather than as 'curses' or 'spells') is treated as a belief rather than a reality, heavily implying that it is to be treated as a delusion or (in accordance with the 1999 *Praenotanda*) a false opinion. Furthermore, the

---

[76] Rowiński 2011: 83–4.   [77] Rowiński 2011: 110.   [78] Young 2016: 238.
[79] Service National de la Pastorale Liturgique et Sacramentelle 2017: 14.
[80] Église Catholique de France 2017.

French bishops share the concern expressed by some exorcists (as we shall see further in the text) that the witchcraft hypothesis undermines both personal freedom and personal responsibility.

The exorcists whose attitudes and approaches are considered later have worked in Italy, Spain, the United Kingdom, Lithuania, and the United States. A notable and regrettable absence from this sample is an exorcist from the developing world, for the reason that the writings of Catholic exorcists from the developing world were not available to this researcher, and it is hard to gauge the extent to which exorcists in these regions write about their own practice. The dearth of publications on demonology from exorcists in the developing world may be down to more limited publication opportunities; less than 1 per cent of global publishing occurs in Africa, for example.[81] However, it is also possible that the genre of exorcists writing about their practice – begun in Europe by Gabriele Amorth – is of limited importance in cultural contexts where demonic activity, witchcraft, and exorcism are accepted by many Catholics as normal aspects of life.

'Exorcism literature' in the developed world is educational (informing the public about the ministry of exorcism and dispelling misconceptions) but also apologetic, justifying the ministry of exorcism and the reality of demonic threats to a public assumed to be broadly sceptical about, or disengaged from, spiritual matters. However, such literature is popular worldwide and not just in the developed world – the writings of Amorth, the most influential modern exorcist, have been translated into multiple languages and are available in developing countries, while José Antonio Fortea's writings are available in Spanish-speaking South America. The Spanish and Latin American publishing industries remain closely interconnected,[82] perhaps with the result that there is less demand for South American writings on exorcism and demonology when Spanish authors are available. However, it is also possible that the apparent silence of exorcists from the developing world owes more to structural inequalities that favour the publication of the writings of European and North American exorcists than to variations in the demand for exorcism literature, and this is an area where more research is required.

4.1 Fr Gabriele Amorth on Witchcraft

Gabriele Amorth (1925–2016), exorcist of the archdiocese of Rome, was for many years one of the world's best-known Catholic exorcists, and there can be little doubt that Amorth was the most influential Catholic exorcist of modern times, as well as the most widely read and translated. Amorth was an outspoken

---

[81] Raju et al. 2020: 369–81.   [82] Navarro 2018: 66–84.

figure who presented himself as the church's leading exorcist, giving regular interviews to the media since he believed the ministry of exorcism ought to be publicized rather than kept hidden by the church. Amorth was the first president of the International Association of Exorcists, founded by him and other priests in 1992, which provides training for exorcists in Rome and elsewhere.[83] Amorth's first book on exorcism, *Un Esorcista Raconta* (1990), translated into English as *An Exorcist Tells His Story*, set out his philosophy of exorcism, in which witchcraft played an important role.[84]

In 1990, Amorth was writing in the light of the rubrics of the still-authorized Roman Rite of exorcism of 1614; when the new rite of exorcism was promulgated in 1999, Amorth was highly critical of the liturgy and the *Praenotanda* governing its use.[85] During Amorth's lifetime, the media had a tendency to exaggerate the exorcist's status and importance on account of his link with the archdiocese of Rome. However, Amorth was appointed Rome's diocesan exorcist by Cardinal Ugo Poletti, Vicar General of Rome (the cardinal entrusted with the care of the archdiocese of Rome by the Pope, who can have little directly to do with the running of his diocese) and was never officially an advisor to the Pope or the Vatican on exorcism. Amorth's opinions on exorcism were the private opinions of a practising exorcist, albeit a very influential one, and never represented the church's 'official' view.

Interest in witchcraft is particularly intense among Italian exorcists, of whom Amorth was the best known, perhaps partly because folk religion and belief in witchcraft and curses remain very much part of Italian life. The Dominican friar Moreno Fiori (1959–2011) even devoted an entire book to the subject in 2005. In Fiori's view, witchcraft always involved some worship of Satan because the witch must invoke Satan in order to work malefic harm.[86] Amorth took a similar view, describing witchcraft as 'Directly or indirectly ... a cult of Satan.' Amorth included witch doctors, spiritualists, and mediums as witches,[87] although he was open to the idea of clairvoyance and willing to receive the spiritual insights of 'sensitives'. He defined an evil spell as 'causing the suffering of others through the intervention of the devil', for example, through 'binding', the evil eye, or a curse.

Amorth claimed that sorcery was the most common cause of possession, complaining, 'I do not understand the reasons behind the refusal of some churchmen who claim not to believe in sorcery.'[88] Clearly, Amorth was unaware of the strong Catholic tradition of scepticism about witchcraft stretching into the seventeenth century and beyond. Nevertheless, Amorth himself

[83] Young 2016: 223–4.   [84] Amorth 1999.   [85] Grob 2007: 142–3.   [86] Fiori 2005: 202.
[87] Amorth 1999: 143.   [88] Amorth 1999: 57.

evinced some scepticism, arguing that 'Instances of true sorcery are a minute percentage among the wholesale deceit that prevails in this arena', and that sorcery relies to a large extent on 'suggestions and whims of feeble minds'.[89]

Amorth considered 'spells' and witchcraft to be two different kinds of cursing, identifying four different kinds of curses in total: black magic, curses, the evil eye, and spells.[90] Black magic, in Amorth's view, did not involve 'the use of particular objects' (the *maleficalia* of the 1614 rubrics) but was the attempt to inflict a curse 'by magic formulas and rituals', including the so-called black mass. A simple curse, according to Amorth, was when someone (usually a blood relative) called down evil on someone with words 'spoken with true perfidy', while the evil eye was 'a true spell', but one cast through the sense of sight (although Amorth was doubtful he had ever encountered a true case of the latter). Spells, malefice, or hexes were, however, the kind of curse Amorth believed to be the most common and were inseparable from the making of *maleficalia*. An object created for the purpose of *maleficium* was 'a tangible sign of the will to harm . . . offered to Satan to be imprinted with his evil powers'. In this respect, *maleficalia* were perverse parodies of the sacraments, 'an outward sign of an inward grace',[91] and their power derived from 'contagious magic'.[92]

It was not the objects themselves, according to Amorth, which caused harm but 'the will to harm through demonic intervention', which was imprinted on objects through 'black magic formulas that are chanted while mixing this material'. *Maleficalia* could either be mixed with a person's food to be ingested (in which case the possessed person might later vomit them up during exorcism) or they could be objects external to a person. Amorth credited the influence of the exorcist of the archdiocese of Palermo, Matteo La Grua (1914–2012) for his views regarding *maleficalia*. For La Grua, external *maleficalia* could be either cursed items belonging to a person or 'dolls, puppets, animals, even real people of the same age and sex' that acted as 'transfer material' for a curse. Amorth also called this (which historians and anthropologists know as sympathetic magic) 'imitative magic'.[93] The 'transfer material' may then be stuck with pins or bound, depending on the result intended by the witch.[94] Amorth reported that *maleficalia* such as 'colored threads, tufts of hair, tresses, wooden or iron slivers, rosaries or ribbons tied with the tightest of knots, puppets, animal shapes, blood clots, or pebbles' were often found when the pillows of persons troubled by demons were examined.[95] These items were sometimes invisible to begin with, Amorth claimed, but 'materialized' when a pillow or mattress was sprinkled with holy water.[96]

---

[89] Amorth 1999: 58.   [90] Amorth 1999: 129.   [91] Amorth 1999: 129–32.
[92] Amorth 1999: 145.   [93] Amorth 1999: 144.   [94] Amorth 1999: 133–4.
[95] Amorth 1999: 71.   [96] Amorth 1999: 135.

Another important influence on Amorth was the exorcist Candido Amantini, to whom Amorth was apprenticed early in his ministry. Amorth claimed to have learnt the important lesson from Amantini that *maleficalia* must always be blessed before they are destroyed, otherwise the curse may transfer itself to the exorcist. On one occasion, Amantini was told by a demoniac that the *maleficalia* were in a small wooden box buried under a tree. Amantini accordingly dug up the box, covered its contents with alcohol and burnt it, but not before touching the cursed objects without blessing them. As a consequence, Amorth claimed that Amantini was confined to his bed for three months with severe stomach pains, which continued intermittently for a decade.[97]

Amorth did not go into much detail regarding the precise effects of witchcraft, in contrast to the exorcist of the archdiocese of Fermo, Raul Salvucci, who specified that witchcraft primarily affects the head and acts on a person primarily when they are sleeping and at their most vulnerable. Witchcraft disrupts sleep and thereby wears its victims down.[98] Salvucci believed that ingested *maleficalia* were more effective than *maleficalia* simply placed in proximity to a victim, because when they were inside the body they were always close to the person and their 'negative influences' were therefore stronger.[99]

In spite of his extraordinary claims, Amorth presented himself as a sceptic regarding witchcraft: 'Hexes are always rare', he insisted, and when people believed themselves to be under a curse the cause was usually psychological. Furthermore, curses were often ineffective against those who were protected by a life a prayer, and those who were paid to cast them were often actually swindlers rather than real witches.[100] By making some gestures towards scepticism and insisting that bewitchment had nothing directly to do with *maleficalia* in and of themselves, Amorth pre-emptively shielded himself from charges of superstition. The involvement of an exorcist in cases of cursing was necessary, Amorth argued, because a powerful curse almost always resulted in demonic oppression or possession.[101] At the very least, 'the victim of witchcraft . . . will feel a great aversion for all that is sacred' and will experience misfortunes.[102] However, the destruction of *maleficalia* offered no guarantee of effectiveness against demonic oppression if a hex had already done its work.[103]

Amorth's practice of exorcism was clearly grounded in Italian popular religion as much as in theology, and the exorcist was clear that he considered people consulting witches and sorcerers to be a greater spiritual danger than the threat posed by witches and sorcerers to the innocent.[104] Indeed, Amorth's crusade was as much directed against the fraudulent financial extortions of service

---

[97] Amorth 1999: 139.   [98] Salvucci 1999: 132–3.   [99] Salvucci 1999: 136–7.
[100] Amorth 1999: 135.   [101] Amorth 1999: 137.   [102] Amorth 1999: 145–6.
[103] Amorth 1999: 139.   [104] Amorth 1999: 140–2.

magicians and occult practitioners as against the powers of darkness. Amorth saw the potential financial gain of sorcery as closely linked with its reliance on demonic power.[105] Amorth's crusade was also one against Italian popular religion. He described protective charms and amulets such as 'hairs of badgers, teeth of wolves, or red horns' as 'objects that, even if they are not "charged" with negativity through magical rituals, have ties to Satan through the sin of superstition'.[106] Amorth's demonology was a practical one that emerged from the pastoral exigencies of ministry in an Italian context.

In his foreword to the American edition of Amorth's first book, Fr Benedict Groeschel was perhaps thinking of the exorcist's emphasis on witchcraft and curses when he observed that Amorth 'writes ... in ways quite foreign to the ideas of the English-speaking world' and that Amorth 'uses a rhetoric foreign to most of us and even theological concepts alien to our way of thinking'.[107] Certainly, while Amorth's emphasis on the danger of witchcraft as allegiance to Satan is an idea found among exorcists and demonologists in the English-speaking world, his ideas about cursing and the evil eye (in particular) are culturally specific to the Catholicism of Italy and the Mediterranean. Yet, as we shall see in the case of Vincent Lampert, Amorth's ideas have since gained considerable acceptance among exorcists in the English-speaking world.

4.2 Fr José Antonio Fortea on Witchcraft

The Spanish priest Fr José Antonio Fortea Cucurull (b. 1968), who was the diocesan exorcist of the diocese of Alcalá de Henares (Madrid), is a prolific writer on demonology and the author of *Summa Daemoniaca* (2008), a complete treatise on the theory and practice of exorcism presented in the question and answer form of a medieval theological *summa*.[108] Fortea's work thus differs significantly in form from Amorth's books, which are largely collections of anecdotes interspersed with the exorcist's reflections on demonology and the threat posed by witchcraft. Fortea adopts a much more systematic approach, treating witchcraft in the third part of his 'Treatise of demonology', under the heading 'The work of the demon in man and nature'. Within this, Fortea deals with witchcraft through eight questions:

41. What is witchcraft?
42. Is witchcraft effective?
43. What to do in a case of witchcraft?
44. What is a spell?
45. Does the way of performing witchcraft or a spell matter?

---

[105] Amorth 1999: 144.   [106] Amorth 1999: 148.   [107] Amorth 1999: 7.   [108] Fortea 2008.

46. What is the difference between white magic and black magic?
47. Do magicians divine the future by the intervention of a demon?
48. Does a demon intervene in horoscopes, tarot, and other forms of divining the future?[109]

Fortea's definition of witchcraft (*maleficio*) is 'an operation carried out with the aim of damaging another with the help of demons'. Witchcraft is effective only when permitted by God, and those who invoke demons in order to harm others do so in vain unless God has decided to test someone by allowing such a thing. In Fortea's view, it is impossible to know whether someone is a victim of witchcraft unless they display the signs of possession or other signs 'visible to the exorcist'; however, 'It is also possible to deduce that an evil is the result of witchcraft when that evil is accompanied by evil preternatural events.'[110] Like Amorth, Fortea distinguishes between witchcraft and spells, defining a spell (*hechizo*) as 'any operation carried out for the end of obtaining something positive with the help of demons', in contrast to witchcraft (whose intent is always harmful).[111]

'It may seem logical', Fortea observes, 'that someone who voluntarily opens a door to the devil is possessed, but it may seem stranger for someone to be possessed by witchcraft. That is, by someone who has performed a rite to make him possessed or to kill him'. However, Fortea emphasizes that possession affects the body and not the soul. No act of witchcraft can harm anyone without God's permission; consequently, it cannot be said that any rite of witchcraft causes someone's death or possession: 'If God does not permit it, nothing will happen.' Nevertheless, since innocent people can be possessed, witchcraft must exist, and Fortea concludes that God permits the rites of witches to be effective as a punishment or test for the faithful,[112] even if a bewitched person can easily protect themselves by invoking God's protection: 'Good is always stronger than evil.'[113]

A person's belief that they are the victim of witchcraft is not, in and of itself, grounds for an exorcism; instead, the person should pray the rosary, read the Gospels, pray regularly, attend mass, place a blessed crucifix or image of the Virgin Mary in their home, or sprinkle the home with holy water. However, if witchcraft produces 'influence' on a person the exorcist should step in. If witchcraft has produced an illness it should be treated by conventional medicine before the exorcist becomes involved.[114] In contrast to witchcraft, spells (*hechizos*) pose a threat primarily to those who become involved with demons in order to cast them. Objects used to lay curses or cast spells should be destroyed if they

---

[109] Fortea 2008: 61–8.   [110] Fortea 2008: 61–2.   [111] Fortea 2008: 64.
[112] Fortea 2008: 155–6.   [113] Fortea 2008: 63.   [114] Fortea 2008: 63–4.

are found during the course of exorcism, 'but if they are not encountered it does not matter, since prayer to God destroys all influence which the demonic object may possess'.[115]

Fortea argues that the material or object used to lay a curse or cast a spell is irrelevant, as is the form of conjuration used by a magician; all that really matters, and what gives the curse or spell its effect (if God permits it) is the invocation of a demon. *Maleficalia* are, for Fortea, a demonic deception; demons want people to believe that their power resides in objects, meaning that people will always be under demonic influence as long as they are close to or in contact with such objects. By using specific rites that provoke fear, witches maintain control of the situation. Fortea is critical of exorcists who ascribe 'excessive importance' to the materials and rites used, whether by magicians and witches or by the exorcist himself – perhaps a sideswipe at the Italian exorcists who follow in the footsteps of Amorth. Faith, and the name of Christ, is all the exorcist truly needs in his arsenal.[116]

Fortea is frank about the process by which he came to his unusually sceptical view regarding *maleficalia* (compared with other exorcists). He confesses that, although he initially came to the work of an exorcist believing the rites and materials of witchcraft did not matter, experience as an exorcist caused him to change his mind:

> I considered that there was some kind of unknown relationship between certain material objects and the spirit. That is to say, that having or not having any human material (nails, hair or menstrual blood, for example) from the person against whom the curse is going to be directed was not indifferent. Nor was it indifferent that the evil object (the one with which the curse has been directed) is burnt in the event that it is found.

This change in approach, Fortea believed, was simply a recognition 'that there are much more complex relationships between the material and the spiritual than we imagine, all of them governed, not by irrationality, but by a rationality that surpasses us'. After three years holding this view, however, Fortea changed his mind again. He found himself unable to believe that the specific rites or object used in witchcraft mattered at all and considered this a demonic deception:

> It is the demons that try to make us believe that it matters. Demons are more interested in attacking a person if they are invoked in a certain way, under certain rituals or using certain materials. In themselves, the rituals are indifferent, but hell wants to convince us that they are not, in order to create a kind of 'science of witchcraft' (*ciencia maléfica*). The only thing that matters in

---

[115] Fortea 2008: 64.   [116] Fortea 2008: 64–5.

the effectiveness of a curse are two things: the will of the one who lays the curse and who invokes the demons, and the will of the demons when attacking a person.

Fortea concludes that 'There is no formula to perform a curse, just as there is no formula to perform a miracle'. Everything depends on the will of the operator and the permission of God.[117]

Fortea's approach to witchcraft stands apart from other exorcists, and especially from Amorth's thinking, in Fortea's emphatic rejection of a doctrine of demonic influence through *maleficalia*. He rightly observes that Amorth and other exorcists give no detailed theological or philosophical account of exactly how it is that *maleficalia* cause demonic vexation, and how an object can become cursed. While Fortea formally admits the possibility of witchcraft, his view of the subject allows no independent power to the witch and portrays the witch as the devil's dupe, tricked into believing they are a possessor of magical power when all they are really doing is invoking a demon who is permitted to work evil by God.

In addition to his attack on the mythology of *maleficalia*, other noteworthy features of Fortea's approach to witchcraft are his emphasis on the exorcist as an investigator and his warning that complete certainty is impossible where claims of witchcraft are concerned. In Fortea's view, the faithful can protect themselves against witchcraft easily, and the threat from witchcraft is primarily psychological; the devil wants us to develop a complex 'science of witchcraft' that fills our lives with fear and distracts us from the worship of God, when in reality these illusions can be dispersed by prayer and faith. Fortea's mixture of nuance and forthright scepticism represents an interesting interpretation of *Praenotandum* 15 of the new rite of exorcism – and perhaps one more faithful to the spirit of the *Praenotandum* than the commentary of other exorcists – but it may ultimately emerge from a centuries-old Spanish tradition of ecclesiastical scepticism regarding witchcraft. The Spanish church, as we have seen earlier, has a well-established tradition of treating witchcraft as demonic deception rather than as a direct spiritual threat embodying genuine occult power.

4.3 Fr Jeremy Davies on Witchcraft

The English priest Jeremy Davies (b. 1935) was, along with Amorth, a founder member of the International Association of Exorcists and exorcist of the archdiocese of Westminster. However, Davies's approach to magic and witchcraft reflects different perceptions of the occult among Catholics in the English-speaking world, compared with Mediterranean Europe. For Davies, 'occult

---

[117] Fortea 2008: 66.

practices' are first and foremost forms of occultism and esotericism such as Spiritualism, yoga, astrology, reiki, enneagrams, acupuncture, and any practices deemed part of the 'New Age' movement. The primary risk posed by these practices, in Davies's view, is that those drawn to them will be deceived into believing they are beneficial when they are in fact spiritually harmful.[118] Davies describes one case in which witchcraft was the cause of a possession through a woman reading books about it.[119] However, it seems likely that Davies is here referring to Neo-Pagan witchcraft as a religious and spiritual practice rather than witchcraft in the traditional sense as the projection of harmful occult power.

Nevertheless, Davies insists that 'in cases of curses or witchcraft' it may be necessary for the exorcist to break a 'bond' before proceeding to exorcism, suggesting that the spiritual bonds created by witchcraft and curses are distinct from the demonic influence brought in by witchcraft.[120] Furthermore, Davies acknowledges the reality of *maleficalia*, noting that 'water and other material things ... can ... through witchcraft and other practices, convey curses'. He advises that sprinkling such objects with holy water and throwing them away (without the need for exorcism) should be sufficient.[121] Like Amorth,[122] Davies is inclined to see 'addiction' to divinatory practices in psychological rather than supernatural terms, decrying people's waste of their God-given abilities on 'auto-suggestion'.[123]

4.4 Fr Arnoldas Valkauskas on Witchcraft

The Lithuanian priest, academic and military chaplain Arnoldas Valkauskas (b. 1961), an exorcist in the archdiocese of Kaunas, holds views on witchcraft and curses that contrast somewhat with the views of Amorth, Fortea, and Davies, and represent a more cautious approach to the issue that is focussed on opposition to superstition and encouraging personal responsibility and repentance. In a 2012 commentary on the 1975 document *CFD*, Valkauskas was critical of 'people without healthy faith' who regard the exorcist as a kind of magician. Valkauskas insisted that exorcism is not about intimidating either demons or people but about proclaiming the victory of Christ.[124] The exorcist noted that, as a result of the Soviet occupation of Lithuania, the theological debates about the devil that followed the Second Vatican Council did not take place in the country; on the other hand, Valkauskas believed Lithuania had yet to fully recover from the lingering spiritual impact of atheist Communism.

---

[118] Davies 2009: 17–19.   [119] Davies 2009: 29–30.   [120] Davies 2009: 41.
[121] Davies 2009: 45.   [122] Amorth 1999: 149.   [123] Davies 2009: 19.
[124] Valkauskas 2012: 28.

Valkauskas was particularly critical of those who seek to blame demons for the consequences of their own sinfulness,[125] an attitude that he made clear in a 2018 interview where he included people who believe themselves to be under a curse. Without denying the possibility of the reality of curses, the exorcist took the view that most people who claimed to be cursed did so through a lack of faith, since they were trying to blame someone else for their misfortunes or sins. Only someone who was guilty of grave sin, Valkauskas insisted, could fall victim to a curse in the first place.[126] Valkauskas has attributed the tendency of contemporary Lithuanians to seek out sorcerers (*būrėjai*) to a human desire to flee the freedom offered by faith in God by delegating that freedom to another authority.[127] The greater threat, for Valkauskas, originates not from witchcraft itself but from unchecked superstition and lack of faith. Compared with Amorth, Fortea, and Davies, Valkauskas's views seem more closely aligned with the theology embodied in *Praenotandum* 15 of the revised rite of exorcism, whereby the threat posed by superstition (a false belief in witchcraft and curses) outweighs any threat from witchcraft itself.

4.5 Fr Vincent Lampert on Witchcraft

Vincent Lampert (b. 1963) is an exorcist of the archdiocese of Indianapolis in the United States and one of the most prominent North American exorcists. In his book *Exorcism: The Battle against Satan and His Demons* (2020),[128] Lampert attributes 'a resurgence of magic and things centering on the occult' to a growing gap between the human person and God caused by unbelief.[129] He associates the particular kind of demonic activity known as 'infestation' with witchcraft and curses, noting that 'Infestation connected with an object has to do with items that may have been cursed or those that are used in occult practices, such as a voodoo doll'. In dealing with such infestations, Lampert advises a prayer of blessing as well as an additional prayer 'asking God to break the connection with the demonic', followed by the destruction of the object whenever it is 'associated with magic'. Lampert also associates demonic vexation with curses, arguing that those who are weak in faith are vulnerable to 'the actions used against them to cause harm, using magic'.[130] In such cases, the exorcist should declare 'As a priest of Jesus Christ, I hereby declare null and void any curses, spells, or hexes that may have been placed upon you'.[131]

---

[125] Valkauskas 2012: 28.   [126] Pocytė 2018.   [127] Valkauskas 2012: 28.
[128] Lampert 2020.   [129] Lampert 2020: 6.   [130] Lampert 2020: 33–4.
[131] Lampert 2020: 35.

Questions regarding witchcraft and curses are part of the 'intake question-naire' recommended by Lampert, to be completed by individuals seeking exorcism.[132] Lampert also asks about objects in a person's possession which belonged to another person involved in the occult (in an attempt to detect potential *maleficalia*).[133] A curse, according to Lampert, is when someone or something is 'commended to the devil', in a procedure that is the opposite of commending someone or something to God in blessing: 'To curse means to do harm to another with the help of the devil.' Like Valkauskas, however, Lampert believes that only the weak in faith are vulnerable to curses, which exploit the cracks in a person's spiritual life.[134] Lampert classes the entire 'world of the occult' under the heading of magic, arguing that demonic power is the source of all power and knowledge displayed through everything from astrology to tea leaf reading, Spiritualism, herbs, and crystals.[135] He rejects as demonic decep-tion any suggestion that mediumistic abilities might come from the medium rather than from the co-operation of demons, and takes the view that when people consult mediums a relationship with a demon is formed that allows evil influences into a person's life.[136]

Lampert's is a very extreme view in the light of Catholic tradition; in the Middle Ages, there was much debate among theologians and canonists on the permissibility of astrology, the carrying herbs, and even amulets,[137] while in the twentieth century theologians such as Alois Wiesinger, Herbert Thurston, and Corrado Balducci advocated the view that many 'occult' phenomena should be explained in parapsychological terms as the result of innate human abilities retained after the Fall but only rarely actualized.[138] Indeed, even Amorth avowed the influence of Balducci's thinking on demonology even if he did not trust Balducci's advice on exorcism.[139] By making the category of 'magic' extremely broad and attributing all magic to demonic power, Lampert is argu-ably in danger of making it impossible for the church to engage constructively with popular religion, as well as diluting the meaning of 'magic' beyond a meaningful category. Lampert conflates occultism, Satanism, and folk magical practices, writing them all off as demonic and risking encouraging a paranoid fear of demons behind any form of divination or alternative spiritu-ality. In this respect, Lampert displays considerably less nuance than his exor-cist colleagues in cultures rooted in popular religion; it is difficult to imagine an exorcist in Italy taking as hard a line against all forms of unofficial 'magical' folk religion as Lampert does, not least because the exorcist's work would never be done.

---

[132] Lampert 2020: 110–11.   [133] Lampert 2020: 114.   [134] Lampert 2020: 90–1.
[135] Lampert 2020: 82.   [136] Lampert 2020: 83–4.   [137] Young 2016: 90.
[138] Young 2016: 206–7.   [139] Amorth 1999: 15.

5 Catholicism and Witchcraft in the Developing World

This section will consider and interpret a small number of mentions of witchcraft in the developing world in statements from recent popes and will deal with the issue of witch-hunting by Catholic clergy and lay associations in Africa. The section will also consider the extraordinary case of Emmanuel Milingo, archbishop of Lusaka, whose controversial exorcisms of the bewitched in Zambia resulted in his recall to Rome and the birth of an exorcism cult centred upon Milingo in Italy. The Milingo case, which showed it was perfectly possible to transplant an African exorcism cult into 1990s Catholic Europe, challenges any notion of the 'otherness' of belief in witchcraft in the developing world and suggests that European and African responses to fear of witchcraft are not always entirely dissimilar. Nevertheless, belief in witchcraft is culturally marginal for most people (and even for most Catholics) in Europe and North America, with a few regional exceptions. In large parts of the developing world, by contrast, witchcraft is part of everyday experience for many.

This cultural asymmetry creates specific challenges for the Catholic church in regions such as sub-Saharan Africa and Papua New Guinea, where questioning the reality and power of witchcraft may seem absurd to many people. By failing to engage with the problem of witchcraft, and not offering ordinary Catholics spiritual aid against it, the church in these regions risks its popular credibility. At the same time, bishops and priests who do engage with witchcraft risk the censure of a Vatican bureaucracy still largely governed by prelates from the developed world. Clergy are thus caught between local culture and the hierarchy of the church and face unenviable choices with significant pastoral implications.

Ronald Hutton has argued that, by preaching against the cults of ancestor spirits, nineteenth-century missionaries in Africa may have enhanced the importance of belief in witchcraft as a remaining explanation for misfortune,[140] a phenomenon sometimes described as 'the modernity of witchcraft'.[141] While missionaries were unwilling to accept any claimed benefits of African traditional religion, they were often more than happy to embrace Africans' belief in witchcraft because it confirmed the spiritual darkness in which they believed Africa was plunged and promoted a colonially useful stereotype of superstitious Africans.[142] Missionaries in Africa and other regions where belief in witchcraft was deeply rooted in the culture always faced a choice between combatting belief in witchcraft as dangerous superstition and accepting that the prevalence of witchcraft was real in 'heathen' societies – thereby providing confirmation of people's need for the Christian faith.

---

[140] Hutton 2017: 30.   [141] Werbner 2011: 199.   [142] Waters 2019: 179.

Often, however, Catholic missionary discourse on witchcraft in the developing world seems to elide condemnation of the *practice* of witchcraft and *belief
in* witchcraft, regardless of the failure of logic such elision seems to imply. In
most African cultures, the existence of witchcraft functions as a conspiracy
theory to account for evil events, and while people may identify themselves as
experts in combatting witchcraft, they do not willingly identify themselves as
witches.[143] The status of witch is, in other words, an etic category imposed on
people in large parts of Africa rather than an emic category of self-definition. It
therefore makes little sense to warn simultaneously of the dangers of witchcraft
and to deny its existence. However, it seems likely that the reason such a double
discourse of scepticism and condemnation has arisen in missionary commentary is the use of 'witchcraft' as a catch-all term for all magic and occult activity,
including counter-witchcraft. Demonologists unfamiliar with African culture
may refer to all African magical practices as 'witchcraft', an approach that runs
the danger of giving credence to the real existence of conspiracies of malefic
witches alongside the obvious reality of magical practitioners in general. Since
people accused of witchcraft sometimes face the possibility of death in sub-
Saharan Africa, Papua New Guinea, and elsewhere, the potentially disastrous
(and deadly) consequences of a lazy elision of occult beliefs by European and
American commentators should be obvious.

A recurring theme in the writings of European demonologists is a sense that
the witchcraft of the developing world is somehow different from (and more
powerful than) the rarely encountered witchcraft of Europe. Amorth insisted
that 'the toughest curses' came from Brazil or Africa,[144] and described the
difficulty of exorcizing people 'who are periodically struck by new spells' from
witch doctors. 'Sometimes', Amorth confessed, 'the problem is so complex that
I do not know where to start'.[145] Jeremy Davies displays the same tendency to
regard the struggle against spiritual evil in Africa as different from that in
Europe, recounting how a Ghanaian catechist told him that converts experi-
enced countless attacks 'from the water spirits and household gods and other
pagan demons' before they were able to 'come through to the peace of
Christ'.[146] As noted earlier, the absence of accessible demonological writings
by exorcists in the developing world hampers the study of Catholic approaches
to witchcraft in these regions on the same terms as we have approached the
attitudes of exorcists in Europe and America. The researcher is instead reliant
on the outsider perspectives of western anthropologists. More study of the
attitudes of Catholic bishops' conferences in the developing world is needed

---

[143] Waters 2019: 180.   [144] Amorth 1999: 148.   [145] Amorth 1999: 114.
[146] Davies 2009: 23.

to give a proper understanding of how the hierarchy of the church interacts with witchcraft belief in regions where it is a prominent cultural feature.

5.1 The Popes on Witchcraft in the Developing World

Modern papal pronouncements have dealt with witchcraft solely in the context of the developing world. On the few occasions when he mentioned witchcraft, Pope John Paul II seemed to condemn belief in it while elsewhere implying its reality. Speaking in the capital of Papua New Guinea, Port Moresby, at a mass for the sick on 8 May 1984, the pope underlined that suffering is not caused 'by witchcraft or evil spirits'.[147] However, on a visit to Tanzania on 4 September 1990 the pope asked Tanzanians whether 'the human dignity of all individuals [is] always respected? Or is it threatened by practices such as *uchawi or witchcraft*, which lead those who are involved in it to forms of enslavement and false worship?'[148] In this latter statement, witchcraft is not a false belief but a dangerous practice that threatens human dignity – something in which people are really involved rather than an imagined threat. Furthermore, the Swahili word for witchcraft used by John Paul II on this occasion, *uchawi*, has the specific meaning of harmful witchcraft in Tanzanian society.[149]

For Pope Benedict XVI, the key to dealing with the problem of witchcraft belief in the developing world was understanding its nature and origins, and the German pope clearly saw such belief as a result of imperfect adherence to the Christian faith. On 29 October 2011, Pope Benedict addressed the bishops of Angola and São Tomé and Príncipe on the problem of belief in witchcraft in Africa, portraying it as a relic of attachment to traditional religion, and urging bishops to speak up on behalf of those falsely accused of witchcraft:

> The second reef in your work of evangelization is the hearts of the baptized are still divided between Christianity and traditional African religions. Afflicted by problems in life, they do not hesitate to resort to practices that are incompatible with following Christ . . . . An abominable effect of this is the marginalization and even the killing of children and the elderly who are falsely condemned of witchcraft. Remembering that human life is sacred in all its phases and situations, continue, dear Bishops, to raise your voice on behalf of all its victims.

Pope Benedict went on to urge deeper study, 'in the attempt to determine the deep reason for such practices, to identify the pastoral and social risks conveyed by them and to arrive at the method which leads to their definitive eradication, with the cooperation of the Government and of civil society'.[150] Indeed, Pope

---

[147] John Paul II 1984.   [148] John Paul II 1990.   [149] Malefakis 2019: 51–66.
[150] Benedict XVI 2011.

Benedict's belief that witchcraft deserved further study is also testified in his earlier writings as Cardinal Joseph Ratzinger; in 1983 he contributed a foreword to a book by Cardinal Suenens, *Renewal and the Powers of Darkness*, in which Ratzinger bemoaned the lack of examination of witchcraft among Catholic demonologists, in contrast to the Protestant churches:

> Among [Protestant] literature there is an enormous wealth of information on the devil and his acolytes, on witchcraft and its methodology and so forth. In the Catholic Church, this field has been left almost fallow. Our directives for specific pastoral response are inadequate for our times.[151]

Like his predecessor John Paul II, Pope Benedict was not altogether clear on whether witchcraft was to be condemned as a false belief or as a real practice, and while it seems highly unlikely that Benedict intended his call for the 'eradication' of 'practices' of witchcraft as an invitation to witch-hunting, the pope's use of language was lacking in clarity when dealing with a culturally sensitive matter.

Pope Benedict expanded on some of the ideas aired to the Angolan and São Toméan bishops in the post-synodal exhortation *Africae Munus* ('The Gift of Africa') of 19 November 2011, where Benedict underlined the roots of witch-craft in African traditional religion, but once again failed to distinguish between witchcraft itself and practices designed to ward it off:

> Witchcraft, which is based on the traditional religions, is currently experien-cing a certain revival. Old fears are re-surfacing and creating paralyzing bonds of subjection. Anxiety over health, well-being, children, the climate, and protection from evil spirits at times lead people to have recourse to practices of traditional African religions that are incompatible with Christian teaching. The problem of 'dual affiliation' – to Christianity and to the traditional African religions – remains a challenge. Through profound catechesis and inculturation, the Church in Africa needs to help people to discover the fullness of Gospel values. It is important to determine the profound meaning of these practices of witchcraft by identifying the many theological, social and pastoral implications of this scourge.[152]

'Practices of witchcraft' in *Africae Munus* appears to have the meaning of 'practices in some way associated with belief in witchcraft'. By insisting on conflating witchcraft with belief in witchcraft, *Africae Munus* comes across as distinctly confusing, a product of European anxiety about popular religion and belief in Africa that is neither accompanied by much understanding of African belief nor informed by an understanding of earlier Catholic debates about witchcraft and belief in witchcraft. While Pope Benedict was a little more

---

[151] Suenens 1983: 79–80.   [152] Benedict XVI 2011: §93.

engaged with the problem of witchcraft in the developing world than his predecessor, it remained a low priority and even, perhaps, a source of some embarrassment. When visiting the faculty of theology of the University of Kinshasa in 1987, the future Pope Benedict proposed seminars on the validity of orders and the species consecrated in the eucharist, focussing on the challenge posed by Protestant groups as the principal issue of 'Africanizing' the church. The challenge of dealing with belief in witchcraft received no mention at all.[153]

So far, Pope Francis's only comment on witchcraft was in an Angelus address of 17 November 2013, where the pope warned against 'false "saviours" who attempt to replace Jesus: worldly leaders, religious gurus, even sorcerers, people who wish to attract hearts and minds to themselves, especially those of young people'.[154] Clearly, such a statement against sorcerers can be interpreted either as a warning against their genuine magical power or merely as a warning of the psychological power they exert in societies where belief in sorcery is widespread. Overall, the last three popes have given the impression of wanting to condemn the excesses of belief in witchcraft (such as murders of people accused of being witches), but they have remained reluctant to condemn belief in witchcraft outright. Whether that reluctance stems from concern about the pastoral challenges faced by African bishops is less clear, but it is likely that a clear and straightforward condemnation of belief in witchcraft as a superstitious delusion would be both controversial within the church, and might discredit the Catholic church in large parts of the developing world.

5.2 Catholic Witch-Hunters in Africa

In a study of the Tooro region of Western Uganda, Heike Behrend described how the Catholic church failed in imposing a 'top-down' Africanization in response to the Second Vatican Council, and found itself losing adherents to sects who were more willing to engage with 'the most pressing spiritual interests of many Catholics – healing and protection from witchcraft'. In 1981, however, a sister and brother of the Holy Cross brought the Catholic charismatic renewal to the region, and campaigns of healing and witch-hunting were taken forward by lay Catholic organizations such as the Ugandan Martyrs Guild (UMG) and the Legion of Mary. The UMG began its 'crusades' against witches in 1995, accusing people of cannibalism or of transforming themselves into animals. After the beating of one elderly woman accused of witchcraft, shape-shifting, and cannibalism in the course of a 'crusade', such activities were

---

[153] Douglas 1999: 190.   [154] Francis 2013.

forbidden by the church, but the 'crusades' continued in a non-violent form under the leadership of an American priest.

The UMG's non-violent crusades continued to draw on a vocabulary of warfare and involved house-to-house searches of a village for *maleficalia* and evidence of cannibalism, which were then collected, photographed, and burned in front of the local church while members of the UMG preached; the crusade was concluded with a celebration of mass, indicating the sanction of the local church. The UMG's new approach to witches and cannibals was to offer them healing, since they were not considered wholly responsible for their demonically inspired actions. Supposed 'cannibals' were encouraged to confess who they had eaten, as well as giving the names of other cannibals so that, as in the witch trials of early modern Europe, an ever-expanding list of suspects could be interrogated.[155]

In Behrend's view, while the UMG contributed to the proliferation of belief in cannibals, witches and occult forces, the UMG also contained anti-witchcraft violence by offering 'cannibals' the chance to confess and be reintegrated into their communities, since most people accused confessed and were largely accepted thereafter – indeed, many 'ex-cannibals' swelled the ranks of the UMG. The UMG deployed a logic of 'mutual outbidding' of evil powers that ensured their leaders 'constantly gave proof of dangerous evil forces to show their superior power'. The UMG thus simultaneously invented the problem of witch-cannibalism and provided the solution for it, but in doing so provided communities with a sense of unity and purpose as well as, potentially, reintegrating some marginalized people into the community.

However, according to Behrend the UMG's approach failed 'to establish a self-reliant Christian person', diminishing the importance of personal responsibility by emphasizing 'the permanent threat of outside satanic forces, because only through fighting these forces could [Catholics] give proof of their own powers'.[156] While the exact nature of the Catholic priesthood and the hierarchy's involvement in 'crusades' against witches in Uganda is not entirely clear from Behrend's research, at the very least clergy condoned the activities of lay witch-hunters and, at most, were complicit in it. However, given the church's earlier condemnation of the UMG's original acts of anti-witchcraft violence, the church's accommodation of non-violent witch-hunting may have been a concession designed to limit the threat of violence posed by the UMG.

Like Behrend, in their study of Catholicism among the Dagomba people in northern Ghana, the anthropologists Vincent Boi-Nai and Jon Kirby argued that the church can succeed only if it provides solutions to the problems Africans

---

[155] Behrend 2007: 50–2.   [156] Behrend 2007: 53–4.

actually experience (including witchcraft), by substituting Catholic versions of non-Christian rituals: 'If Catholicism is to offer a path to advancement and religious change, to peace and security, to an integrated African identity on the global scene, it must once again learn to see the unseen by new rituals.'[157] The nature of African religion, Boi-Nai and Kirby argue, is practical problem-solving and evangelistic activity does not and cannot eliminate beliefs such as witchcraft. One Ghanaian priest interviewed by the anthropologists complained that the church lacked the resources to deal with the problems Africans considered important, leaving them in the hands of non-Christians because Christians were forbidden from dealing with such matters. Furthermore, the church was unable to stop accusations of witchcraft. As one priest interviewed by the anthropologists lamented, 'Every year there is a witchcraft case and we cannot do anything about it. These old ladies are innocent, most of them are falsely accused but what can the Church do to save them?'[158]

While the church may not be doing enough to acculturate to African conditions, including the development of Catholic versions of rituals considered necessary to solving everyday problems with invisible causes, it is noteworthy that some of the Catholic anti-witchcraft activity identified by Behrend, Boi-Nai, and Kirby was initiated not by Africans, but by priests from the United States. Indeed, the anthropologist Mary Douglas argued that, in the case of the Lele people of Zaire (now the Democratic Republic of the Congo), western missionary activity largely *created* fear of witchcraft. In the late 1940s, the European priest in charge of the mission of the Oblates of Mary Immaculate (OMI) at Mapangu fulminated against 'paganism' and any involvement with the rites of ancestral religion. By the late 1980s, the former ancestral monotheism of the Lele had been transformed into a kind of dualism, in which the god of their ancestors was identified with the devil of Christianity and any manifestations of ancestral religion were seen as sorcery.[159] The missionaries failed 'to see anything that was good in the old Lele religion that could be salvaged'.[160]

In 1976, a Catholic movement known as Kimvuku was launched among the Lele by the Oblates of Mary Immaculate, whose avowed purpose was 'to stop the officiants of the old religion from intimidating the villagers by threats', but was widely interpreted as an anti-sorcery cult by the Lele themselves. When a young Lele priest, ordained in 1978, declared himself able to identify sorcerers and heal by laying on hands, the Kimvuku movement quickly degenerated into a witch-hunting campaign (the Mupele cult) in which *l'abbé* (as the priest was known) went from village to village torturing, extracting confessions from and

---

[157] Boi-Nai and Kirby 1998: 549.   [158] Boi-Nai and Kirby 1998: 547.
[159] Douglas 1999: 178–9.   [160] Douglas 1999: 180.

exorcizing accused witches. When the papal nuncio in Kinshasa finally got word of what was happening he conferred with the diocesan bishop and two of the leading Mupele priests were sent abroad, but a climate of fear remained.[161] While western missionary priests were not directly responsible for the violence perpetrated by the Mupele cult, Douglas held them indirectly responsible because they created the necessary conditions for the cult, especially by insisting on demonizing indigenous religion. Furthermore, simply removing the witch-finding priests did not solve the problems created by the missionaries.

While the post-conciliar church was ostensibly committed to Africanization, Maia Green has argued (in a study of the Tanzanian diocese of Mahenge) that the post-conciliar focus on the laity's understanding of the foundations of faith undermined the effectiveness of acculturation in contexts where Catholicism was hitherto regarded as 'a system of practices through which the person can experience God'. The changes wrought by Vatican II 'served to undermine the supernatural authority of Catholicism', which was 'exposed as something manufactured, an artefact of humanity'. The diocese of Mahenge discourages priests becoming involved in healings or exorcisms, but the priests' refusal to drive out spirits (even though the people believe they have special abilities to see spirits and witches) is interpreted as selfish and further discredits the church.[162]

This analysis raises the question of what Africanization means, and what value it has, if it fails to engage with those problems considered important by Africans. As Gerrie Ter Haar observed, the modern church faces the paradox that, while it still relies for its very *raison d'être* on supernatural claims, it nevertheless often presents its faith and activities in de-supernaturalized language: '[The church] has opted for the Western scientific view of the world, [but] as a religious body it has almost by definition to leave room for metaphysical explanations, including beliefs that appear to pre-date modern science.'[163] While walking a tightrope between rationalism and supernaturalism may appeal to some in Europe and America, this strategy yields no discernible benefit for the church in cultures where the supernatural and preternatural are unquestioned aspects of life.

5.3 A Clash of Cultures: The Milingo Affair

The story of Emmanuel Milingo (b. 1930), archbishop of Lusaka in Zambia, who was summoned to Rome on account of his claims to cure witchcraft and ended up conducting a successful ministry as an exorcist in Italy, is one of the most intriguing episodes in modern religious history. Vatican discipline against

---

[161] Douglas 1999: 184–7.   [162] Green 2003: 53.   [163] Ter Haar 1992: 191.

Milingo, which was ostensibly the triumph of a more cautious and measured European Catholic approach to witchcraft over the excesses of an African prelate, backfired spectacularly when Milingo proved immensely popular in Italy, in 'a spectacular inversion of missionary activity'.[164] While Milingo's subsequent disassociation from the Catholic church, and eventual excommunication, weakened the significance of his legacy as an African Catholic rebel against western demonological preconceptions, this episode in which a senior cleric went on a campaign of exorcism in the heart of the Catholic church remains a troubling one for the Vatican that raises many questions about the process of acculturation and the church's approach to witchcraft.

Milingo was consecrated archbishop of Lusaka and primate of Zambia in 1969 by Pope Paul VI, making him one of the most senior Catholic clerics of southern Africa. Giordana Charuty has characterized Milingo as a prelate who sought to implement the Second Vatican Council's agenda of acculturation by celebrating African culture in the church's liturgy and rites. However, Milingo encountered the opposition of missionaries who envisaged a Zambian Catholicism closer to European models. Yet, Milingo went further than mere acculturation when, in July 1973, he declared he possessed a personal ability to cure *mashawe*, a form of possession by evil spirits that many believed was caused by witches. In 1976, Milingo was invited to the United States to visit a charismatic community at Ann Arbor, Michigan, which further inspired him to stage public contests between the Holy Spirit and evil spirits in Zambia.[165]

On 12 September 1982, the British journalist David Willey (the paper's Rome correspondent) reported in *The Observer* that accusations of 'witchcraft' had been levelled at Archbishop Milingo, which were the cause of his being summoned to Rome. Milingo himself traced the accusations of witchcraft against him to the papal pro-nuncio in Lusaka, Archbishop Giorgio Zur (1930–2019). Gerrie Ter Haar has suggested that the pro-nuncio and other church officials viewed Milingo as a 'witch-doctor', but the accusation of witchcraft was presented vaguely in the western press in terms of wizardry, tribal magic, 'voodoo', and animism. The Zambian press emphatically rejected any accusations of witchcraft against Milingo, but at the same time these accusations plausibly explained why the archbishop had been recalled to Rome.[166] In reality, Gerrie Ter Haar has argued, it was Archbishop Zur and the Zambian bishops' concern about becoming embroiled in an exorcism scandal (in the wake of the death of Anneliese Michel in 1976) that caused them to sanction Milingo.[167]

---

[164] Charuty 2013: 98.   [165] Charuty 2013: 97.   [166] Ter Haar 1992: 61–2.
[167] Ter Haar 1992: 191.

Ter Haar argued that the supposed accusation of witchcraft levelled against Milingo by Vatican officials, if such a thing ever took place, was 'little more than a metaphor for the Western Church's lack of understanding when faced with the identity of the African Catholic Church'.[168] The alleged witchcraft accusation became the basis for framing the conflict between Milingo and the Vatican in terms of western racism, both in the western and the Zambian press, but as Ter Haar has noted there was 'a Babel-like confusion of speech' since 'witchcraft' meant something totally different to westerners and Zambians. While witchcraft for Zambians was the real projection of evil, and not to be confused with other cultural practices (including counter-witchcraft), for westerners it was 'a simplistic metaphor' for the Vatican's alleged view of Africa. In the western press, 'witchcraft' was 'shorthand for anything to do with life in Africa and with being black and backward'.[169] However, the mention of witchcraft in relation to Milingo's ministry, even if Zambians did not believe the archbishop was a witch or a witch-doctor, generated anxiety in the Zambian government, which was keen 'to suppress every reminder of old beliefs considered backward or unhelpful to the building of a modern nation'.[170]

In the light of so much confusion, it is difficult to determine exactly what role a battle against witchcraft played in Milingo's ministry. At the time of Milingo's recall to Rome western newspapers reported that Milingo's failure to follow the prescribed liturgy of exorcism had given rise to Rome's accusations of 'witchcraft' against him, which here served as a synonym for superstitious practices.[171] Mona MacMillan, who edited Milingo's own testimony about the affair, argued that Milingo shared the same aim as the missionaries who wanted to free people from fear of *mashawe*, but whereas the missionaries thought they could 'teach Africans sense', Milingo understood the importance of working with the grain of African beliefs to achieve liberation from evil.[172]

Milingo insisted that his expertise in dealing with witchcraft came from experience: 'I have talked with the witches', he declared, 'and I have dealt with the dead'. In the archbishop's view, poverty and a desire for success drove people to make pacts with the devil.[173] Furthermore, 'To be an agent of the devil is a rank which cannot be disputed', and the demonically possessed could be expected to point out or identify the witch who had harmed them when subjected to exorcism.[174] Milingo associated bewitchment with being put into a trance by a spell sent from a witch and held that spells that came from witches and from the devil could be distinguished. According to Milingo, 'A witch, in the strict sense of that word, is a person who has the

---

[168] Ter Haar 1992: 62. [169] Ter Haar 1992: 70 [170] Ter Haar 1992: 226.
[171] Ter Haar 1992: 62. [172] Milingo 1984: 5. [173] Milingo 1984: 36–8.
[174] Milingo 1984: 45.

power – and it is a massive power – to use what is commonly known as black magic.' A witch was a disciple of the devil, a 'devil incarnate' in whom 'morality does not exist'. Witches refused healing prayer and inherited their 'formation' as witches.[175]

On arriving in Rome in 1982, Milingo was tested by psychiatrists and interviewed by the Cardinal Prefect of Propaganda Fide, the Secretary General of the Congregation for the Evangelization of Peoples and others. The curial officials questioned Milingo about his addition of unauthorized prayers (and praying in tongues) during the rite of confirmation, as well as his encouragement of the practice of anointing by the laity in Zambia. Finally, on 6 July 1983, Milingo managed to secure an audience with Pope John Paul II, who told him the Zambian bishops would not allow him to return because Milingo's vocation was for healing and not for governing his archdiocese. The pope promised the church would safeguard Milingo's 'healing apostolate', and in return, Milingo agreed to resign as archbishop of Lusaka.[176]

Milingo chose to interpret the pope's promise to safeguard his healing ministry as general permission to perform services of charismatic healing and exorcism, which proved immensely popular in Italy and in Rome itself. Milingo's frank attitude to witchcraft struck a chord with Italian Catholics who may have been frustrated by their own clergy's reluctance to engage with the issue. An 'exorcism cult' rapidly developed around the Zambian archbishop, who made appearances on Italian television and routinely filled large venues in Rome and surrounding cities with ecstatic crowds, some of whom publicly displayed apparent signs of demonic possession. However, rather than simply importing African spirituality to Italy, Vittorio Lanternari argued that Milingo's appeal in Italy was a re-awakening of slumbering cultural trends that in fact united Zambia and Italy:

> The advent of Milingo in the midst of Italian culture, far from constituting a radical innovation, points up and revitalizes an archaic mentality already officially removed, but only partly hidden and one that has been resurrected in official circles by the last two popes [Paul VI and John Paul II] with their proclamations that re-evaluate the role of Satan in human society. All Milingo's faithful in fact relive … the atmosphere of former centuries, of medieval and Renaissance times, that links our culture with that of traditional African society. In this respect it seems appropriate to talk of the relationship Milingo has with popular Italian culture, of a 'short circuit' between two energy poles in contact, from which flames that are capable of starting a fire burst forth.[177]

---

[175] Milingo 1984: 99.   [176] Milingo 1984: 135–7.   [177] Lanternari 1998: 271.

On this interpretation, Milingo was simply giving Italian Catholics what they really wanted but their clergy had been denying them, and the subsequent expansion of exorcism in Italy in the 1990s and thereafter seems to bear out Lanternari's analysis. Italy and Africa were not as different as they seemed.

Milingo's techniques were also practised by his Italian priest disciples. When a twenty-four-year-old woman in the Italian city of Taranto (known as T) approached her parish priest, it turned out that he was a follower of the Zambian archbishop. The priest diagnosed the woman's anorexia, migraines, and dizziness as caused by witchcraft; an acquaintance of T, the priest claimed, had cast a spell on her. Assisted by a lay faith healer, the priest proceeded to an exorcism of T that was witnessed and recorded by an anthropological researcher, Anna Maria Albano. On another occasion, a woman approached the same priest suffering from insomnia, anxiety, anorexia, and unexplained noises at night. The woman confessed to having procured 'recipes and instruments' from a witch to bewitch her daughter-in-law. The priest declared that the woman had submitted to Satan and proceeded to exorcize her.[178] This use of exorcism as a remedy not only for witchcraft but also to deliver people from *being* witches was distinctly African, even though all of the participants in these rituals were white Italians.

Milingo's tendency to see Satanic conspiracies and his accusations of Satanism against high-ranking figures in the church proved too much for Rome in 1996, when Milingo's exorcisms in Milan caused Rome to ban the archbishop from further public healing ministry.[179] Although Gabriele Amorth was already actively promoting exorcism in the early 1990s, it seems likely that Milingo's Italian campaigns of exorcism contributed to the intensification of interest in possession, witchcraft, and exorcism in Italy – either under the actual influence of Milingo's exorcism cult or (more likely) in reaction to it, as a response to the demand for deliverance that Milingo revealed. This renewed emphasis of the Italian church on exorcism led in turn to the growth of demonological literature written by Italian exorcists. As such, it is difficult to overstate the importance of the Milingo episode, both for the development of the contemporary ministry of exorcism in Italy (and therefore the rest of the world, since Italian exorcists are so influential) and for Rome's dealings with local churches in the developing world.

6 Conclusions

On a theological level, the 'witchcraft hypothesis' (the idea that demonic activity can be provoked against a person by a third party) is sustained by the

---

[178] Lanternari 1998: 275–6.   [179] Lanternari 1998: 264–6; Young 2016: 226–7.

need to explain how innocent people can come to be demonically possessed or otherwise troubled by evil spirits. This was an idea that emerged in the late Middle Ages and reached the apogee of its influence in the sixteenth and seventeenth centuries. Between the eighteenth and twentieth centuries, however, the Catholic church largely drew back from the idea of witchcraft to the point where it became a dead letter even if few theologians explicitly denied the possibility of witchcraft. However, the more explicit demonological scepticism of the 1960s and 1970s produced a counter-reaction in the 1980s that created a 'neo-demonology' that often strongly affirms the reality of witchcraft.

The sources of Catholic 'neo-demonology' can be found in Leo XIII's belief in Satanic conspiracies, the rise of Satanic Ritual Abuse mythology, and the influence of the charismatic renewal. Late twentieth-century neo-demonology was disconnected both from the scepticism of eighteenth- and nineteenth-century Catholic writing on demonology and from the writings of earlier twentieth-century theologians who were prepared to consider parapsychological rather than demonological explanations. Neo-demonology emerged almost in a vacuum of tradition, in the aftermath of the perceived collapse of traditional demonology in the post-conciliar era. The neo-demonologists have a tendency to define witchcraft (*maleficium, veneficium*) very broadly, to the point where it loses much meaning and may refer to any involvement with the occult. However, contemporary Catholic writers on demonology generally show little interest in the idea of a formal Satanic pact or in the idea of witches as a devil-worshipping cult (key elements of the late medieval witchcraft mythology), although they portray witches as generally beholden to the devil.

Witchcraft is a minority interest among Catholic theologians, perhaps because it is considered a distasteful or fringe subject (in spite of its prominence in many world cultures), but the lack of engagement with the problem of witchcraft means that it is a matter left to the exorcists, a largely closed cadre of self-proclaimed experts who have a vested interest in sustaining the belief that witchcraft poses a genuine threat. As the delegated experts of their diocesan bishops, diocesan exorcists enjoy an official status within the church even if their writings on witchcraft represent their personal views. Some exorcists avow scepticism and caution with regard to witchcraft, but this performative scepticism may be a rhetorical strategy of legitimation for the authority of the exorcist; after all, a perception of excessive credulity might undermine the demonologist's authority. A feature of contemporary Catholic demonological writing on witchcraft is a tendency to slide effortlessly between two apparently conflicting discourses: one focussed on condemning 'superstition' and excessive belief in witchcraft, and another condemning the practice of witchcraft itself.

The scant pronouncements of popes in relation to witchcraft have similarly dabbled in both of these discourses. Pope Benedict XVI was rightly concerned about whether there was sufficient understanding in the church of the phenomenon of witchcraft in the developing world. There are troubling questions about whether the church has the anthropological resources to effectively evangelize cultures and peoples where belief in witchcraft plays a major role in everyday life. Largely written or heavily influenced by Italian exorcists such as Amorth, the small academic literature on practical demonology represents an Italocentric approach to witchcraft and cursing whose relevance to cultural contexts in the developing world is questionable. This literature informs and distorts Vatican attitudes towards witchcraft in world cultures where witchcraft is a significant problem but where there is little accessible literature on the subject produced by exorcists – perhaps because there is simply no need to write apologetically on a subject accepted as a normal part of life by so many.

It is inescapable that the church's one public intervention in the hierarchy of an African nation to excise an anti-sorcery cult – the recall of Emmanuel Milingo to Rome in 1982 – was a dramatic failure. It is unclear to what extent Rome is able to impose an official view of witchcraft on local churches, and more research is needed in this area. However, anthropologists such as Mary Douglas have argued that the theological emphases of Vatican II and its aftermath hampered Catholicism's ability to deal with witchcraft: 'In this arena, confronting and explaining something evil, post-Vatican II theologians have little to say.'[180]

A tension exists between exorcism as an ancient ministry of the church and its inevitable corollary of demonology, which is always culturally conditioned and culturally and geographically contingent. Demonologists and exorcists must decide between responding to their cultural context and its specific concerns, or imposing an external theological understanding of spiritual evil. When they pursue the latter course, a question arises about the applicability of alien concepts of evil to cultures where a different idea of witchcraft exists; it is hard to assert with confidence, for example, that Catholic Italians who fear the evil eye and Catholic Ugandans who fear cults of cannibal sorcerers are responding to the same phenomenon. There is also a tension between church authorities who establish the rules for exorcism and exorcists as practitioners; the church maintains a 'polite fiction' that exorcism is a liturgical matter, when in reality exorcism is as much a charismatic practice that constitutes a battleground between church authorities and a group of self-proclaimed

---

[180] Douglas 1999: 190.

experts who are not always willing to accept episcopal authority and are sometimes, as in the case of Amorth, scathing of the church hierarchy.[181]

In theory, the hierarchical nature of the church should mean that exorcists have little or no control over the rules governing their craft, but the 2011 authorization of the *Rituale Romanum* of 1614 by the pontifical commission *Ecclesia Dei* effectively hamstrung the efforts of the Sacred Congregation for Divine Worship to introduce a new rite of exorcism with new rubrics. While the authorization of the 1614 rite of exorcism may have been an inevitable consequence of *Summorum Pontificum* and the authorization of the 'extraordinary form' in general, it represented a victory for the exorcists over the liturgists since it re-authorized not only the old rite of exorcism but also (it would seem) its rubrics dealing with witchcraft and *maleficalia*.

While some contemporary exorcists show no sign of taking seriously the cautious approach of the 1999 *Praenotanda* towards witchcraft, in some cases there has been a shift towards a more 'psychological' interpretation of curses and a reluctance to identify malefic witchcraft as a cause of supposed demonic vexation. On the other hand, exorcists are very willing to identify witchcraft (in the broad sense of magic and involvement in the occult) as a cause of demonic activity. Yet the contemporary Catholic church has so far failed to grapple satisfactorily with the problem of witchcraft, derogating the issue to the theological judgement of a more or less reliable professional cadre of exorcists. These exorcists have shown a tendency to yield uncritically to a historically uninformed 'neo-demonological' orthodoxy, which is worryingly disengaged from a well-established Catholic tradition of scepticism regarding witchcraft that reaches back into the seventeenth century. Theological consideration of witchcraft has so far failed to attract sufficient theological resources, perhaps because it is perceived as a problem of the church in the developing world (although the popularity of Milingo's ministry in Italy and the evidence collected by Giordan and Possamai in southern Europe suggest this is not actually true). This is a state of affairs that reflects poorly on the Eurocentrism of the institutional church.

In addition to the need for systematic theological exploration of the 'witchcraft hypothesis' by Catholic theologians, there is a strong case for future research into the church's institutional approach to witchcraft in the developing world. The work of anthropologists, while valuable, should be supplemented by systematic research into the authorization of exorcisms and anti-witchcraft measures by ecclesiastical hierarchies in the developing world. While clerical attitudes to witchcraft in Europe and America can be studied (at least in part)

---

[181] Amorth 1999: 171.

from the writings of exorcists, there is little corresponding literature on clerical attitudes and approaches in the developing world, where anthropologists have tended to focus on popular movements rather than on the institutional church. Furthermore, the unusual quantitative work of Giordan and Possamai, while it provides a snapshot of contemporary Catholic witchcraft belief in southern Europe, should be built upon through further studies of the ongoing prevalence of belief in witchcraft in societies where it is often wrongly presumed to be marginal (or to have died out entirely). The study of contemporary Catholic approaches to witchcraft is a fertile field for theologians, sociologists, and historians of religion to which this Element offers the briefest of introductions.

Abbreviations

CCC	*Catechism of the Catholic Church*
CDC	*Codice di diretto canonico e leggi complementari.* Rome: Coletti, 2007.
CFD	Congregation for the Doctrine of the Faith (1975). Christian faith and demonology. *L'Osservatore Romano*, English edition, 10 July 1975, 6–10.
DEOD	*De exorcizandis obsessis a demonio* in Sodi, M. and Flores Arcas, J. J., eds. (2004). *Rituale Romanum editio princeps (1614)*. Vatican City: Libreria Editrice Vaticana.
DESQ	*De Exorcismis et Supplicationibus Quibusdam*, 2nd ed. Vatican City: Typis Vaticanis, 2004.
SNPLS	Service National de la Pastorale Liturgique et Sacramentelle

References

Amorth, G. (1999). *An Exorcist Tells His Story*. San Francisco, CA: Ignatius Press.

Bailey, G. and Peoples, J. (2013). *Essentials of Cultural Anthropology*, 3rd ed. Stamford, CT: Wadsworth.

Bamonte, F. (2006). *Possessioni diaboliche ed esorcismo: como riconoscere l'astuto ingannatore*. Rome: Paoline editoriale libri.

Baroja, J. C. (1990). Witchcraft and Catholic theology. In B. Ankarloo and G. Henningsen, eds. *Early Modern European Witchcraft: Centres and Peripheries*. Oxford: Oxford University Press, pp. 19–43.

Behrend, H. (2007). The rise of occult powers, AIDS and the Roman Catholic church in western Uganda. *Journal of Religion in Africa*, 37, 41–58.

Boi-Nai, V. and Kirby, J. P. (1998). Catholicism and problem-solving in Dagbon. *Social Compass*, 45, 533–5.

Cameron, E. (2010). *Enchanted Europe: Superstition, Reason, and Religion, 1250–1750*. Oxford: Oxford University Press.

Charuty, G. (2013). L'africaniste en Italie: le cas Milingo. *Archives de sciences sociales des religions*, 161, 93–111.

Clark, S. (1997). *Thinking with Demons: The Idea of Witchcraft in Early Modern Europe*. Oxford: Oxford University Press.

Conferenza episcopale della Toscana (1995). *A proposito di magia e demonologia: nota pastorale*. Florence: Cooperativa Firenze 2000.

Congregation for Divine Worship and the Discipline of the Sacraments (2004). *De Exorcismis et Supplicationibus Quibusdam*, 2nd ed. Vatican City: Typis Vaticanis.

Congregation for the Doctrine of the Faith (1975). Christian faith and demonology. *L'Osservatore Romano*, English ed., 10 July 1975, 6–10.

Davies, J. (2009). *Exorcism from a Catholic Perspective*. London: Catholic Truth Society.

Davies, O. (1999). *Witchcraft, Magic and Culture 1736–1951*. Manchester: Manchester University Press.

De Blécourt, W. (1999). The witch, her victim, the unwitcher and the researcher: The continued existence of traditional witchcraft. In W. De Blécourt, R. Hutton, and J. La Fontaine, eds. *Witchcraft and Magic in Europe, Volume 6: The Twentieth Century*. London: Athlone, pp. 143–219.

Douglas, M. (1999). Sorcery accusations unleashed: The Lele revisited, 1987. *Africa: Journal of the International African Institute*, 69, 177–93.

Favret-Saada, J. (1977). *Les Mots, la Mort, les Sorts*. Paris: Gallimard.

Fiori, M. (2005). *Il maleficio: indagine sulle pratiche del male*. Rome: Città Nuova.

Fortea, J.-A. (2008). *Summa Daemoniaca: Tratado de Demonología y Manual de Exorcistas*. Madrid: Palmyra.

Frankfurter, D. (2008). *Evil Incarnate: Rumors of Satanic Conspiracy and Satanic Abuse in History*. Princeton, NJ: Princeton University Press.

Giordan, G. and Possamai, A. (2018). *Sociology of Exorcism in Late Modernity*. Basingstoke: Palgrave MacMillan.

Goodman, F. D. (2005). *The Exorcism of Anneliese Michel*, 2nd ed. Eugene: Resource.

Green, M. B. (2003). *Priests, Witches and Power: Popular Christianity after Mission in Southern Tanzania*. Cambridge: Cambridge University Press.

Grob, J. S. (2007). A major revision of the discipline on exorcism: A comparative study on the liturgical laws in the 1614 and 1998 rites of exorcism. PhD thesis, St Paul University, Ottawa.

Halsted, C. (2020). 'They ride on the backs of certain beasts': The night rides, the Canon *Episcopi*, and Regino of Prüm's historical method. *Magic, Ritual and Witchcraft*, 15, 361–85.

Hutton, R. (2017). *The Witch: A History of Fear, from Ancient Times to the Present*. New Haven, CT: Yale University Press.

Institoris, H. (2009). *The Hammer of Witches: A Complete Translation of the Malleus Maleficarum*. Cambridge: Cambridge University Press.

Jenkins, R. (2014). *Black Magic and Bogeymen: Fear, Rumour and Popular Belief in the North of Ireland, 1972–74*. Cork: Cork University Press.

John Paul II. (2007). *Codice di diretto canonico e leggi complementari*. Rome: Coletti.

La Fontaine, J. (1999). Satanism and satanic mythology. In W. De Blécourt, R. Hutton, and J. La Fontaine, eds. *Witchcraft and Magic in Europe, Volume 6: The Twentieth Century*. London: Athlone, pp. 81–140.

Lado, L. (2009). *Catholic Pentecostalism and the Paradoxes of Africanization: Processes of Localization in a Catholic Charismatic Movement in Cameroon*. Leiden: Brill.

Lampert, V. P. (2020). *Exorcism: The Battle against Satan and His Demons*. Steubenville, OH: Emmaus Road.

Lanternari, V. (1998). From Africa into Italy: The exorcistic-therapeutic cult of Emmanuel Milingo. In P. B. Clarke, ed. *New Trends and Developments in African Religions*. Westport, CT: Greenwood Press, pp. 263–82.

Laycock, J. P., ed. (2020). *The Penguin Book of Exorcisms*. London: Penguin.

Lehner, U. (2016). *The Catholic Enlightenment: The Forgotten History of a Global Movement*. Oxford: Oxford University Press.

Malefakis, A. (2019). *Tanzania's Informal Economy: The Micro-politics of Street Vending*. London: Zed.

Mayneri, C. A. (2016). 'I went out into the street . . . and now I fight for my life': Street children and witchcraft accusations in Bangui (Central African Republic). In M. Pavanello, ed. *Perspectives on African Witchcraft*. London: Routledge, pp. 185–96.

Midelfort, H. C. E. (2005). *Exorcism and Enlightenment: Johann Joseph Gassner and the Demons of Eighteenth-century Germany*. New Haven, CT: Yale University Press.

Milingo, E. (1984). *The World in Between: Christian Healing and the Struggle for Spiritual Survival*. London: C. Hurst.

Nanni, C. (2004). *Il dito di Dio e il potere di Satano*. Vatican City: CEV.

Navarro, J. E. (2018). The Sudamericana publishing house: Catalogs as objects of study. In H. J. Allen and A. R. Reynolds, eds. *Latin American Textualities: History, Materiality, and Digital Media*. Tucson, AZ: University of Arizona Press.

Ndlovu, H. L. (2016). African beliefs concerning people with disabilities: Implications for theological education. *Journal of Disability and Religion*, 1–2, 29–39.

Ostling, M. (2011), *Between the Devil and the Host: Imagining Witchcraft in Early Modern Poland*. Oxford: Oxford University Press.

Pesch, C. (1898). *Praelectiones dogmaticae: Tomus III*. Freiburg: Herder.

Pontifical Commission *Ecclesia Dei* (2012). Prot. N. 39/2011 L. *Agli esorcisti ed ausiliari: lettera circolare*, 54, 9.

Pratt, A. M. (1915). The attitude of the Catholic church towards witchcraft and the allied practices of sorcery and magic. PhD thesis, Catholic University of America, Washington, DC.

Raju, R., Claassen, J., Pietersen, J., and Abrahamse, D. (2020). An authentic flip subscription model for Africa: Library as publisher service. *Library Management*, 41, 369–81.

Ratzinger, J. (1994). Introduction to the Catechism of the Catholic Church. In J. Ratzinger and C. Schönborn, eds. *Introduction to the Catechism of the Catholic Church*. San Francisco, CA: Ignatius Press, pp. 9–36.

Rowiński, T. (2011). *Zawód: Egzorcysta: wywiady z polskimi egzorcystami*. Kraków: Wydawnictwo.

Salvucci, R. (1999). *Cosa fare con questi diavoli? Indicazioni pastorali di un esorcista*. Milan: Ancora.

Seitz, J. (2011). *Witchcraft and Inquisition in Early Modern Venice*. Cambridge: Cambridge University Press.

Service National de la Pastorale Liturgique et Sacramentelle (2017). *Protection, Délivrance, Guérison: célébrations et prières*. Paris: Desclée Mame.

Sluhovsky, M. (2007). *Believe Not Every Spirit: Possession, Mysticism and Discernment in Early Modern Catholicism*. Chicago, IL: University of Chicago Press.

Sodi, M. and Flores Arcas, J. J., eds. (2004). *Rituale Romanum editio princeps (1614)*. Vatican City: Libreria Editrice Vaticana.

Suenens, L.-J. (1983). *Renewal and the Powers of Darkness*. London: Darton, Longmann and Todd.

Ter Haar, G. (1992). *Spirit of Africa: The Healing Ministry of Archbishop Milingo of Zambia*. London: C. Hurst.

Valkauskas, A. (2012). Kelios pastabos dėl dokumento 'Krikščioniškasis tikėjimas ir demonologija'. *Bažnyčios žinios*, 5, 27–8.

Van der Geest, S. (2002). From wisdom to witchcraft: Ambivalence towards old age in rural Ghana. *Africa*, 72, 437–63.

Walker, A. (1993). The devil you think you know: Demonology and the charismatic movement. In T. A. Small, A. Walker, and N. Wright, eds. *Charismatic Renewal: The Search for a Theology*. London: SPCK, pp. 86–97.

Waters, T. (2019). *Cursed Britain: A History of Witchcraft and Black Magic in Modern Times*. New Haven, CT: Yale University Press.

Werbner, R. (2011). The charismatic dividual and the sacred self. *Journal of Religion in Africa*, 41, 180–205.

Young, F. (2016). *A History of Exorcism in Catholic Christianity*. Basingstoke: Palgrave MacMillan.

Young, F. (2017). *Magic as a Political Crime in Medieval and Early Modern England: A History of Sorcery and Treason*. London: I. B. Tauris.

Young, F. (forthcoming). Authorities and control. In A. Sneddon, ed. *A Cultural History of Magic in the Age of Enlightenment*. London: Bloomsbury.

Zocca, F. and Urame, J. (2008). *Sorcery, Witchcraft, and Christianity in Melanesia*. Goroka: Melanesian Institute.

Web Sources

Benedict XVI. (29 October 2011). Address to the Bishops of Angola and São Tomé and Príncipe, www.vatican.va/content/benedict-xvi/en/speeches/2011/october/documents/hf_ben-xvi_spe_20111029_ad-limina-angola.html (accessed 10 May 2021).

Benedict XVI. (19 November 2011). Africae Munus, www.vatican.va/content/benedict-xvi/en/apost_exhortations/documents/hf_ben-xvi_ex h_20111119_africae-munus.html (accessed 10 May 2021).

Église Catholique de France (2017). Exorcisme: accueil, écoute et discerne-ment, https://eglise.catholique.fr/exorcisme (accessed 23 May 2021).

Francis (pope). (17 November 2013). Angelus, www.vatican.va/content/francesco/en/angelus/2013/documents/papa-francesco_angelus_20131117.html (accessed 19 May 2021).

John Paul II. (8 May 1984). Homily at Port Moresby (Papua New Guinea), www.vatican.va/content/john-paul-ii/en/homilies/1984/documents/hf_jp-ii_hom_19840508_incontro-malati.html (accessed 10 May 2021).

John Paul II. (4 September 1990). Homily at Mwanza (Tanzania), www.vatican.va/content/john-paul-ii/en/homilies/1990/documents/hf_jp-ii_hom_19900904_mwanza.html (accessed 10 May 2021).

John Paul II. (1992). Catechism of the Catholic Church, www.vatican.va/archive/catechism_lt (accessed 8 May 2021).

Levada, W. and Pozzo, G. (30 April 2011). Instruction on the Application of the Apostolic Letter *Summorum Pontificum*, www.vatican.va/roman_curia/pontifical_commissions/ecclsdei/documents/rc_com_ecclsdei_doc_20110430_istr-universae-ecclesiae_en.html (accessed 19 May 2021).

Pocytė, K. (22 July 2018). Prakeiksmas yra ne juokai: ar tai tikrovė, ar tik silpnų žmonių baimės?, www.delfi.lt/news/daily/lithuania/prakeiksmas-yra-ne-juo kai-ar-tai-tikrove-ar-tik-silpnu-zmoniu-baimes.d?id=78553369 (accessed 14 May 2021).

Viganò, C. M. (28 October 2020). Interview with BardsFM, https://dryburgh.com/wp-content/uploads/2020/12/Archbishop-Vigano_BardsFM-Interview-October-2020_English.pdf (accessed 26 May 2021).

Winters, M. S. (16 December 2020). The Evangelical-Catholic Alliance Becomes a Conspiracy Theory Carnival, www.ncronline.org/news/opinion/distinctly-catholic/evangelical-catholic-alliance-becomes-conspiracy-theory-carnival (accessed 26 May 2021).

Magic

Marion Gibson
University of Exeter

Marion Gibson is Professor of Renaissance and Magical Literatures and Director of the Flexible Combined Honours Programme at the University of Exeter. Her publications include *Possession, Puritanism and Print: Darrell, Harsnett, Shakespeare and the Elizabethan Exorcism Controversy* (2006), *Witchcraft Myths in American Culture* (2007), *Imagining the Pagan Past: Gods and Goddesses in Literature and History since the Dark Ages* (2013), *The Arden Shakespeare Dictionary of Shakespeare's Demonology* (with Jo Esra, 2014), *Rediscovering Renaissance Witchcraft* (2017), and *Witchcraft: The Basics* (2018). Her new book, *The Witches of St Osyth: Persecution, Murder and Betrayal in Elizabethan England,* will be published by Cambridge University Press in 2022.

About the Series

Elements in Magic aims to restore the study of magic, broadly defined, to a central place within culture: one which it occupied for many centuries before being set apart by changing discourses of rationality and meaning. Understood as a continuing and potent force within global civilisation, magical thinking is imaginatively approached here as a cluster of activities, attitudes, beliefs and motivations which include topics such as alchemy, astrology, divination, exorcism, the fantastical, folklore, haunting, supernatural creatures, necromancy, ritual, spirit possession and witchcraft.

Cambridge Elements$^{=}$

Magic

Elements in the Series

The Strix-Witch
Daniel Ogden

The War on Witchcraft: Andrew Dickson White, George Lincoln Burr, and the
Origins of Witchcraft Historiography
Jan Machielsen

Witchcraft and the Modern Roman Catholic Church
Francis Young

A full series listing is available at: www.cambridge.org/EMGl

Printed in the United States
by Baker & Taylor Publisher Services